"It's wonderful! I loved it!! *the Battle: In Jesus' Name*, in a.m. to finish it. *The Land of the Giants* is more in-depth and took longer, but I could hardly put it down. At the end of every chapter, I stopped and prayed the prayer she prayed in that chapter!"

— *Julia Waggstaff*
Mother, former LVN, intercessor, faithful friend to many

"I finished it! I am in awe, Donna! I love it!!! A wonderful 'Prayer with Power' Primer! Chapters 11 and 12 are life-changing. I am so proud of you, Girl, and our God!!!!"

— *Karen Elliot*
President, San Antonio Day Aglow lighthouse; missionary of short-term trips to India, Russia, Ecuador

"Donna Hamilton's natural and supernatural experiences coupled together as she walks through life here on earth, are Kingdom works that bring our Lord continuous glory and praise in the lives she touches. First, she tells of a real experience or situation in her life. Secondly are the prayers with scriptures, together with brief teachings, that shaped her prayers concerning the situation. Lastly, God hears and answers with supernatural power seen in natural results! I found myself praying her prayers over my situations in my life as I read through her book. Thanks Donna, for writing this powerful book. Concerning your vision, count me in the Delta formation behind you and advancing with you as the General God has appointed you–to take the giants in the land.

— *Dee Ann Chandler*
President, Central Texas Area, Aglow International

"I don't know what I expected when I read your second book. I knew it would be good, but I didn't expect what happened. While I was reading, the Holy Spirit was all over me and all over your book. Oh my gosh! I just cried and cried; the Holy Spirit was so powerful. I read it in one day. I sat at the kitchen table and read the whole thing on my iPad. I've never felt that way about any book. It was just awesome! Then I remembered that years ago, Joan (Luckey) prophesied that you would be teaching people to pray, especially women."

—Lou Skogen
Friend, mother of twelve, prayer-missions veteran, giver, sower, hears from God

"*The Land of the Giants* is excellent! There's no other book like it. I loved every chapter, but I especially liked the part where Donna prayed that she could 'meet a Satanist – a high one!' and the way God answered her prayer. You've got to read this book!"

— Christina Roberts
Surgical technician at Limmer Hair Transplant Center, worshipper of God

"I just finished *The Land of the Giants*. This God-given sequel to *Run to the Battle: In Jesus' Name* is a militant training manual of world-changing prayer, presented like you're Donna's best friend sitting beside her on a sofa! What a treasure penned through her by the Lord, to the body of Christ."

— Taria Vaughn
Mighty woman of God, wife, mother, grandmother, intercessor

"LOVE IT!! I wanted you to know how much I learned by reading your book. Thank you for letting me read it. It is anointed, needed by the body of Christ for encouragement and strengthening of their faith. It will go ALL over the earth! It is that anointed!"

—*Cathy Jackson*
College professor, wife, mother, prayer warrior, gift of helps expressed through servant ministry, friend

"Wow! What a blessing this has been to me. I am calling it my "one-a-day" vitamin. I am trying to read one story a day. It is deep, it is clear; it is an example to me. This is like Sid Roth's mentoring program. Love it! God's richest blessings to you!"

— *Jo Ann Robles*
Wife, speaker, Bible teacher, children's Sunday school teacher

"It's a wonderful book! I pray it goes far and wide in many different languages! I call Donna's books, after the Bible, my 'Holy Spirit manuals.' Donna grabs the word of God and wields it like a Spiritual sword. She teaches and shows us by example how we, too, can practically and powerfully apply the Word to difficult challenges and gain astonishing, even impossible victories, I keep multiple copies of her book *Run To The Battle: In Jesus' Name*, on hand so I can share them with others. I believe God will use *The Land of the Giants* to inspire and equip His people to effectively meet the challenges and opportunities of the days ahead."

— *Brenda Abbatiello*
Former parochial school teacher, home school mother, prayer warrior, prayer group leader

"Thank goodness for Donna Hamilton, my friend and prayer partner for over 35 years. She is a woman of prayer who is teaching the body of Christ how important prayer is to our lives. *The Land of the Giants* is a book of answered prayers and the different situations that set the Father in motion to answer them. This book is thrilling because it shows how interested the Father is in meeting the needs and desires of His children. The call to prayer is the Father's invitation to visit with Him. All Glory to the Risen Lord!"

—Joan Luckey
Pastor; teacher at Teen Challenge; care leader; prayer room leader; GraceLife Church, Lincoln, CA

"This new book by Donna Hamilton brings an inspirational trumpet call to those privileged to serve the Most High in these strategic End Times! Donna models Daniel 11:32b (KJV) *"but the people who do know their God shall be strong, and do exploits."* Example after example showcases ordinary circumstances becoming extraordinary testimonies by obedience, faith and courage. The Word of God clearly directed Donna and will stir the reader to also step out in faith and do exploits!"

—Marie Perusek, M. D.
Diagnostic radiologist, speaker, coordinator of intercessory prayer team for a national ministry, wife, mother

"Upon being asked to provide a reader's review for my dear friend Donna Hamilton's long-awaited book, *The Land of the Giants*, I was torn between savoring every page or reading it as quickly as I had her first book, *Run to the Battle: In Jesus' Name.* Of course, I read it quickly—I couldn't stop turning the pages! It is powerful, impactful, and encouraging! She has outdone herself, and I feel honored to have been among the first to read it. Would I be too forward in asking when the next book comes out?"

—Mary Simmons
Wife, mother, high school band mom,
X-ray technician, gifts of mercy and giving

"Donna, I want to thank for writing this book. It is an amazing faith builder. Your obedience to God in writing it is truly a blessing to countless women and men who read it. It encourages others to step out in faith to do exactly what the BIBLE tells us we should be doing. *The Land of the Giants* will be eye opening for beginning pray-ers as well as seasoned intercessor. Read it and be blessed!"

—Glenda (Withheld)
Prayer warrior for Jesus Christ

The Women Are Coming to

THE LAND OF THE GIANTS

DONNA HAMILTON

Word of Power Printing
San Antonio, Texas

First Edition, First Printing

Published by Word of Power Printing, San Antonio, Texas
Printed and Bound by Lighting Press, Inc., Totowa, New Jersey

Cover Illustration and Design: Monette "Mo" Cavin
Interior Layout: Sarah Hamilton

ISBN: 978-0-9844436-1-1

Contents

Honor is Due

Render therefore to all their due:
taxes to whom taxes are due, customs to whom
customs, fear to whom fear, honor to whom honor.
— Romans 13:7

God has graciously brought wonderful people into my life when I needed encouragement, advice, or assistance in completing *The Land of the Giants* (LOTG). I want to thank Him and them. It has strengthened my belief that He wants this book written and published—that it is part of my "God assignment." To Him be all glory and honor!

I want to thank these special people in the order they entered my life. In 2011, a young woman read my first book, *Run to the Battle: In Jesus' Name*, then purchased three copies; one for her, one for her mother, and one for her mother's best friend, Dee Chandler. Dee was and is President of Central Texas Area (CTA) board, for Aglow International. Aglow is a Christian organization which began 50 years ago in Seattle area with four women praying in a living room—and is now in 170 nations! One day she said, "Dee Chandler wants to meet you." When we met, Dee told me, "I am urging all my presidents to have you as a speaker." Through this, my book received increased exposure over a large area, and I became involved in Aglow again as an officer.

Dee, thank you for all your encouragement and support over the last five years! You lead with wisdom, grace, and creativity and model godly leadership.

As I became busier, writing LOTG gradually halted. At the 2015 CTA Spring Conference, Cathy Jackson of Dallas and Jo Ann Robles of San Antonio said almost the identical thing to me; "I've been waiting three years for your next book. When is it going to be done?" Spurred by this, I finished writing LOTG before the 2016 conference! Cathy, you were so gracious and generous to voluntarily edit the book! You gave many valuable hours editing the punctuation. Your expertise, professionalism and love are valued! Jo Ann, thank you for your continued interest and encouragement! Brenda Abbatiello, thank you for investing so much of your time and effort into the thoughtful comments and suggestions you made! Thank you, dear ladies! Your enthusiasm for my first book was an inspiration for me to finish *The Land of the Giants*!

Thank you to my precious daughter-in-law, Sarah! She has spent countless hours formatting this book for me! She has worked diligently with grace and patience to complete it in a professional and timely manner, all while raising their two wonderful children with Torrey, our son. Thank you for spending late nights on the phone going over formatting, layout, and editing. Your knowledge, skill, and expertise raised this book to a new level. You added beauty to it in so many ways I was ignorant of, but delighted with when I saw it! Truly you are a jewel of great price that adorns our family and blesses Torrey daily. Thank you, Sarah!

Thanks and honor are due to Monette "Mo" Cavin, who painted such a beautiful cover! You have been very patient with me, Mo, as I requested such things as, "Can you make that one lady run in a different direction?" and "Oh, the other woman had blonde hair, not that one!" She has adjusted or repainted many things to more accurately portray the vision God gave me. In the vision, the women were running in to join the army at the back, but it's not accurate to the vision to show the back and the giant together, so I think Mo came up with a great way to show both! It is true to the spirit of it. It takes true talent to "see" someone else's vision and paint it! Thank you, dear Mo, and God bless you, in Jesus' name!

My love and thanks to others also who are not named, but certainly have contributed much to the producing of this book! Taria Vaughn, my prayer partner for 14 years shall be named! I think you all make me understand a little of what God felt when He said, "You are engraved upon My hand."

Throughout the years, my husband, children, and family have been a wonderful support as I have gone on prayer missions and pursued writing and other ministry aspects. Thank you, Ed, Deborah, Laura, Paul, Torrey, and Christina! You are all a gift from God for which I am very grateful!

Sincerely,
Donna Hamilton

FOREWORD

Every since I met Donna Hamilton, I have been intrigued and interested in understanding her relationship with God and have found over the years a true woman of faith, simplicity, a pure heart, and absolute trust in God.

When I first came to know her, I was working on a rental property her son owned and I was dealing with an outside staircase made of steel and cement. It needed reinforcement and to be better attached to the upstairs apartment. It was also bent in some places which I could not repair; it was made of steel and could not be bent with conventional tools.

Donna was watching me work then began to pray "In the name of Jesus, be straightened out and bend back into place!"

I thought, *"This woman's nuts!"* ignored her, and went about my work. The metal did not bend or straighten and later I remonstrated to a friend of mine that there was a woman with false spirituality and making elaborate, meaningless prayers. That's what I thought of Donna when I first encountered her. But I was in for a surprise.

My first surprise came when I told her I was a Christian musician and she said, "Well, I am a Christian writer."

I thought (facetiously), "*Isn't that interesting?*" but she asked me, a stranger and a handyman, if I would like to read her book. I agreed, and in the end I told her I thought she had written a Christian classic, talking about her first book, *Run To The Battle: In Jesus' Name*. I was very much impressed with her book which at that time had not been published.

The next time I met Donna was to collect for some work I had done on the property and drove to her and her husband's home and was received by her into her kitchen in Christian hospitality. I was grateful to be able to sit down and she offered me something to drink. Then from nowhere and instantaneously, I heard the Holy Spirit telling me to confess my sin of domestic abuse to Donna. I knew it was the Holy Spirit, having spent a large part of my life as a charismatic Catholic, and I confessed to this strange woman who tries to bend steel with her prayers (confess your sins to one another that you might grow). Then the Holy Spirit began to speak to me, telling me I was going to be given a second chance. My sin and problems in my life had caused a Gap between me and the Lord's blessings, but that day in the kitchen of a woman who bends steel with her prayers, I was reconciled to my Lord.

Since that time when Donna and I would meet for lunch to discuss her book or what God was doing in our lives, sometimes Ed was with us, sometimes not, I received much blessing and healing with this spiritual woman. Over the years I have come to know her husband, Ed, now of 50 years of marriage, and have met her children and grandchildren.

I am a witness to her solid life in Christ, bearing much fruit, and her ever–growing circle of friends who benefit from her prayers and counsel. I have found her to be a true woman of faith, love, and hope in God.

I have been her creative editor for both books and can share my understanding of her second book, *The Land Of The Giants*. Her first book, *Run To The Battle: In Jesus' Name*, is an important book that inspires one to pray and is very powerful to remind us of prayer and God's power. This second book of hers is more in-depth, how to do it.

She shares her process and approach to prayer which I believe is not only significant to help us learn how to pray, but will be a book that will be studied by students and teachers of prayer for ages to come. I am glad to know Donna Hamilton for what she has done for me and the things she has done for others and, I believe, the world.

— Thomas the Hermit, Thomas Magner
Handyman, anointed musician, contemplative

Introduction

O God, You have taught me from my youth;
and to this day I declare Your wondrous works.
Now also when I am old and gray-headed,
O God, do not forsake me until I declare
Your strength to this generation,
Your power to everyone who is to come.
— Psalms 71:17–18

My daddy loved me and he thought I was beautiful. Daddy could "talk" like Donald Duck, and my brothers and little sister and I would laugh with delight when he would do so. I remember when I was young, he would pick me up and hold me in his arms and people would ask me (a surprising number of them I realize now), "How did you get your name?" Daddy would laugh louder than anyone when I always earnestly replied, "I was named for Donald Duck." My name, of course, is Donna. At that tender age, I never understood why big people always laughed. It took me a long time to realize I was named after Daddy, whose name was Donald—not Donald Duck!

Even though I accepted Jesus when twelve years old and was baptized in the baptistery in the basement of the small Church of Christ building in Fairbanks, Alaska, it was the summer after we moved to Kenai, the summer before my senior year, that I felt God put His hand upon my life. It was through this thought that came to me, *"There has to be more to religion than going to church three times a week and going to parties and dances the rest of the week,"* which I really enjoyed by the way.

After thinking about it (it never occurred to me to *pray* about it), I decided to read a chapter a day in the Bible. Now I recognize that Abba Daddy, God, put that thought into my heart. In spite of going to church every time the doors were open as they say, I didn't have any idea how to start or where to begin. I did have a big black King James Bible which Mother had given me, with the words of Jesus printed in red. I finally decided to read the words written in red, "just the things that Jesus said."

At first it was the last thing I did at night. I remember coming in after a party or dance and being in bed with the light out when I would remember, "Oh, that chapter!" so I'd get out of bed, turn on the light, and read the next chapter, mostly the words in red. Soon, from being the last thing I did at night, reading my chapter for the day became the first thing I did in the morning. On school days while getting ready, I'd lay the Bible open on the bed and read it while I dressed; then prop it up on the top of my dresser and read while I put on my makeup. Soon it wasn't just one chapter, it was two, or three if I could manage it. And I was reading the words in black too.

Then something began to occur that had never happened to me before. When certain situations came up at school, a verse from the Bible, something Jesus said, would just float up in my mind, and I could almost hear the words as though they were being spoken. They always related to what was going on around me.

I remember once standing in the lunch line with my "cool" friends, and quite a ways ahead of us in line was a girl from a "homestead family." (In Alaska, a person could acquire a homestead of 160 acres if they lived on the land a certain number of years and farmed it. Usually homestead families were "broke" or pretty close to it, at least the ones my family had known in Fairbanks.)

One of the girls near me pointed at her and said to the rest of us, "Look at that girl! Look at her dress! Ha ha! It's so ugly!" The girl's dress *was* rather long and shapeless; to me it looked like a homemade, cotton dress. Everyone turned to look, and several started making derogatory comments about it and laughing.

Just like that, clear as a bell I heard in my spirit, *"Judge not, that you be not judged. For with what judgment you judge, you will be judged,"* I don't know if I heard or remembered the rest of it, but the whole thought came to mind, *"for with what measure you mete, it will be measured back to you."* (Matthew 7:1–2), all in the language of the old King James Bible I was reading every morning, except it said "ye" instead of you.

I said, "Let's not talk about her. That might be all she has or all her family can afford," and every one of those girls stopped laughing and we changed the subject. I don't know why that incident is so clear in my memory, but I do know I was surprised at their response to my words. I believe it could indicate we all have greater influence than we realize; also that everyone has a conscience, and when one person speaks out against cruelty or unkindness, it frees others to act with kindness and grace. Also, like you perhaps, I don't want to be judged harshly myself.

As the daily Bible reading of the gospels continued, I found my interest in the dances and parties lessening. Also, when I did go to a dance, I began to observe things I had not noticed or had dismissed before; a girl and a guy leaving together or perhaps two couples leaving together and coming back an hour or two later: inebriated to some degree, faces flushed, the girls' hair messed up, make up gone, etc. A girl at one of the parties became drunk and started puking. The attraction of public dances and private parties in homes lost their "glow" to me. More and more I wanted to be alone with God and my Bible.

Then I remembered a conversation I had had with our minister, Billy Joe Mize, up in Fairbanks *two years* before! Billy Joe had suggested I go to his alma mater, Abilene Christian College (University) in Texas. I had dismissed it, never giving it another thought, until now when that conversation came back to me, with the *name* of the college!

A desire was conceived in me to attend Abilene Christian College. I requested an application, filled it out, and mailed it back. There were no summer jobs available in Kenai by the time school was out, but one of my teachers had invited me and a couple of other girls to visit her in Anchorage for a week after graduation. My parents consented to this, and I flew up there with the understanding that if I could get a job and a place to stay in that week, I could work in Anchorage for the summer. God blessed me; I got a job at the A &W Root Beer stand, and a fine family of the 10th and B Church of Christ invited me to stay with them for the summer. Fortunately, they lived on the same side of town as the A & W. Once or twice they gave me a ride, but generally I walked the mile and a half or so each way to and from work. It was pleasant work: taking orders, fixing fries, bagging them, drawing off foamy mugs of root beer or other soft drinks, and sampling some too, a perk of the job. By the end of summer, I had saved $98 for college and returned to Kenai.

My grandparents, Mom's parents, had driven up the Alcan which is the Alaska-Canada Highway, for the first time that summer. They were down in Kenai, 160 miles south of Anchorage, when Mom called me in Anchorage and told me they had said I could ride with them to California, where I could take a bus from there to Texas. At that point I had not heard from the College on whether I had been accepted or not, so a few nights before we were to leave, I wrote a letter to the Admissions Office of the College. I still remember the heart of what I said:

Dear Abilene Christian College,

It is unusual for one to have to leave for a college far away without knowing if one has been accepted or not because if one waits to learn if he or she has been accepted, one will not have a way to get there.

Jesus said in Matthew 7:7–8, *"Ask, and it shall be given you; seek, and ye shall find; knock, and it shall be opened unto you: For everyone who asketh receiveth; and he that seeketh findeth; and to him that knocketh it shall be opened."* So I am coming, asking for acceptance and trusting it will be given to me; I am seeking entrance, trusting I will find it; and I will be knocking at the door of the College, trusting it shall be opened for me.

> I am leaving here with my grandparents in a few days, going down the Alcan with them to Sacramento, California, and will take a bus from there to Abilene. I hope to hear from you soon that I have been accepted, etc…"

I sealed it and mailed it off with prayers and trust.

That long journey through beautiful country took most of a week. We camped out at night; Grandma and Grandpa slept on a mattress in the back of their old pick up; I slept in the front seat. There was an abundance of wild animals, and it wasn't safe for me to sleep in the open. Grandma cooked over a little Coleman two-burner, propane stove, and I washed the dishes in a wash pan and helped however else I could.

When we arrived at Grandma and Grandpa's house, there was a letter from the College waiting for me which Mother had forwarded. It was a letter of acceptance which also said, "When you arrive at the bus station, call this number, and someone from the College will come for you and drive you to the campus," and included a phone number.

Two days later, Grandpa and Grandma drove me to the Greyhound Bus Station where I bought a one-way ticket to Abilene, Texas. The cost was $44, so I headed out with my Bible, one suitcase, a sack lunch Grandma sent with me, and $54 in my purse.

As we neared Texas and rumbled across it, I was somewhat apprehensive looking out at the prairie, half expecting to see Indians on horseback off in the distance watching the bus. This ignorance shouldn't be too surprising; at the College I was asked by other students if I ate whale blubber and if I lived in an igloo. One young man politely asked, "Where did you learn to speak English?"! The fall of 1962 was not the era of instant communication; letters were used more than telephones for long distance communication.

I had many wonderful experiences at ACC and met many wonderful people. I will share two or three examples of God's close care for me. An older student picked me up at the bus station and took me to someone's home where I stayed for a day or two until the dorms opened. That night was a Freshman Welcome party in one of the buildings. One of the first people I met was Dr. Westmoreland. He asked where I was from; I told him and mentioned I needed to get a job. He asked what my major was going to be. I told him "An English and Journalism major with a Bible minor," also that I had been the editor of our small school newspaper and liked to write.

He said, "You can work for me. I'll give you a job." He was the head of the Journalism Department and needed a student to write a weekly column about the College for the city newspaper! The column was titled "Hilltop Happenings" and had my picture at the top. I have two of the columns. The little bit I earned was applied directly to my tuition.

I was assigned a room in Zellner Hall, the oldest girls' dorm. My roommate, Nancy Walker, was a junior, a tall Texan with a big smile and a bigger heart. We had a room on the bottom floor at the end of the building, the end against which the strong Texas winds blew. Mine was the bed under the window. As winter progressed, it was so cold we taped newspapers over all the windows to block the cold winds.

As the semester continued, I began to run low on personal items such as toothpaste, deodorant, shampoo, etc. and had no money for replacements. However, God had become very real to me, and I was aware of Jesus' words written in red—*"Therefore take no thought, saying, 'What shall we eat?' or, 'What shall we drink?' Or, 'Wherewithal shall we be clothed?' (For after all these things do the Gentiles seek): for your Heavenly Father knoweth ye have need of all these things, But seek ye first the kingdom of God, and His righteousness; and all these things shall be added unto you."* (Matthew 6:31–33, KJV). So as supplies dwindled, I prayed to my Heavenly Father about "these things."

Nancy generously urged me to share her things. I didn't want to, but did use her some of her toothpaste a couple of times before a notice appeared in my mailbox; a package had come for me! It was from my Aunt Fern, Daddy's sister, who lived in Texas. I opened the good-sized box and found a handwritten note from Aunt Fern which said, "Dear Donna June, I was cleaning the bathroom the other day and found extras of some things in the medicine cabinet and under the sink. It occurred to me that perhaps you could use them, so I am sending them to you. Hope you will find some things you can use. Love, Aunt Fern" followed by OOXXOO (Hugs and kisses).

In the box was an assortment of toiletries: toothbrush, toothpaste, soap, shampoo, deodorant, powder, hand cream, and washcloths! God had provided—and my Aunt wasn't even a believer at the time. Praise the Lord!

Christmas break was approaching, and everyone was notified the dorms must be vacant over the holidays; no one could stay on campus. Nancy heard about a store across town that was hiring extra help for the holidays; I applied and was hired for the three weeks school would be out. Nancy worked in the Student Union, called "The Bean," which was going to be open over the holidays. She told her family she wanted to stay in Abilene and work because I was going to be there. She also found a place for us to stay, with "Mom" Henthorne, an 82–year old *saint* who lived about two blocks from the campus.

Mom Henthorne was a small (barely five feet tall) gentlewoman of great Christian character, humor, and wisdom. She was a widow with failing eyesight, so for a number of years she had rented out the larger of the two bedrooms in her charming, small 1930's or 1940's home, to a succession of female students.

Her current boarder, Artheta, a senior, was going home for Christmas and was looking for someone to stay with "Mom" while she was away. Nancy made arrangements for the two of us to stay there while Artheta was gone. I caught a bus a few blocks from the house and rode it across town and back five days a week during the holidays. Nancy and I shared a big double bed in the very pleasant room with its own outside entry; we all shared the one bathroom. There was a covered swing and rose bushes in the backyard. It was idyllic, but I didn't know about the roses or the swing that cold December of 1962.

In January, as the end of the semester approached, I was concerned about whether I was going to be able to stay in college or not. Financially, I was living on a threadbare shoelace! Every time I prayed about the situation, the thought would come, "Go see Mom Henthorne." I didn't want to – I thought that would be like begging, but as the end of the semester drew nearer, I was getting desperate, and that thought wouldn't go away. So one day, while alone in our room, I was on my knees praying about what

I should do, and the thought came again, "Go see Mom Henthorne!"

This time I finally said, "All right, God. I'll go see her, but I'm not going to beg for anything, but I'll go visit her."

The next day I walked to her house and knocked on the door. When she opened the door and recognized it was me, the first words out of her mouth were, "How are you and are you going to be able to stay in college?"

I answered, "I'm fine, but I don't know if I'm going to be able to stay in college or not."

She turned towards the back of the house and called out, "Artheta!" Artheta appeared in the hallway door off the dining room and stood there; I had not met her before. Mom Henthorne said, "Artheta, how would you like to have a roommate?"

Artheta instantly said, "I'd like that," and smiled at me. Mom Henthorne turned and looked up at me with her cloudy blue eyes and said, "You come here next semester and live with me. You and Artheta will share the room." She told me she had been concerned about me, wondering if I was going to be able to stay in school and wanted me to stay there. She said I could earn my keep by doing housework. (I wonder now if she had asked Nancy about my financial situation.)

My responsibilities were to wash the dishes and sweep the kitchen every night. Then once a week on Saturdays, I was to vacuum the whole house; clean the bathroom; take out the trash; dust and polish the furniture; and sweep and mop the kitchen and bathroom floors. For that small amount of work, Mom Henthorne let me share that beautiful, spacious room with Artheta the next semester. It was a blessed time.

Before the semester ended, someone contacted me and asked if I had a way home when school was out, which I didn't. Patsy Hardin, from 10th and B Church of Christ in Anchorage, was a student at Harding Christian College in Oklahoma. She and her fiancé, Ken Smith, wanted to drive to Anchorage together and wondered if I would ride with them, since it was inappropriate for the two of them to travel together for a week when they were unmarried. I accepted immediately. They came to Abilene in Ken's little green Volkswagen, piled up to the back window inside. Ken made about a foot and a half of space in the back seat on the passenger side for me (I was slimmer then), and managed to squeeze in my suitcase with everything else, then we were off for Alaska! It was a great trip. I read through all the letters (epistles) to the church on that trip.

In July, Patsy called from Anchorage and told me a man at the church there was going to drive his van to Oklahoma, and she and Ken, with several other students, were going to go with him. There was room for one more in the van. If I wanted to go, my share of the expenses would be $76. She said the deadline to let them know was a certain date in August several weeks from then.

The summer jobs in Kenai were filled, so, except for babysitting a couple of times for a family from church, I had earned nothing. I spent a lot of time reading the Word and praying. Concerning my return to ACC, I committed that to the Lord saying, "If He wanted me to go back to Abilene, He would need to provide the $76, and I was *not* going to ask my folks for it!"

Two days before the deadline, I got a letter. It was from the Internal Revenue Service. Wondering what the IRS wanted with me, I opened it; inside was a check for $76.80! It was a tax refund from my work at the A &

W the summer before! In January while I was still in the dorm, Daddy had sent a form for me to sign and mail back to him. I realize now that A & W had sent my W-2 form to the house; Daddy had filled out the tax form, and after I signed it and mailed it back to him, he had filed it for me. I had totally forgotten about it; actually I hadn't understood what the form was for and had just done as he said, and here was a check! I called Patsy and told her I would be going!

Someone gave me a ride to Anchorage where, with 5 others, most of us sitting on blankets or sleeping bags on the floor in the back of the van (which had only a front seat!), I was headed down the Alcan again. We took along a picnic cooler and ate peanut butter and jelly sandwiches, cold cereal with milk, and fruit, with little else. I remember only one stop for hamburgers. Mom and Dad paid for my share of the food. Artheta, who had her first teaching job about 50 miles from Lubbock, met me in Lubbock, and drove me to Abilene.

After I arrived, Mom Henthorne told me, "The Lord had told her she was to give me both room and *board* that coming school year."! "Thank You, Jesus!" She also had a new paying boarder, a senior, with whom I shared the room.

I met Ed, my husband, that spring. We married the next year, in the summer of 1965. We have been married 50 years. In fact, today is our Golden Anniversary, August 22, 2015. It is after 11 p. m., so in less than an hour, this day of remembrance will end. We have five excellent children, all married to wonderful people, who love the Lord and ten wonderful grandchildren, two of whom are married and another headed towards engagement. Hallelujah! *"Behold, children are a heritage from the Lord, The fruit of the womb is His reward."* (Psalms 127:3).

We have had many difficult times through the years, but God is faithful. He brought us through them all, though sometimes it took years to recover from the effects of unwise decisions. He has also put wonderful people in our path who have been a blessing to our lives, and through His grace, He's given me many adventures and battles to win in His name with His word and His power. Some are recorded in this book; others are in my first book, *Run To The Battle: In Jesus' Name (RTTB).*

Even though I was taught in the Church of Christ that miracles had ceased with the death of the apostles and those on whom they had laid hands, in 1977 a co-worker in Portland, Oregan, began to talk to me about speaking in tongues, and I was intrigued. A few days later he gave me a copy of *Prison to Praise* by Merlin Caruthers, and after reading that powerful little book, I began to prayerfully study the book of Acts to see if these things were still happening. It took about a year and a half, and in the meantime, the Lord led us to southern California to work with a children's home. We had three children by then, Deborah, Laura, and Paul.

The full story of my receiving the baptism of the Holy Spirit is in my first book, but briefly, in March, 1979, while visiting a full-gospel church in Chino, California, the Lord graciously and dramatically baptized me with the Holy Spirit. Ecstatic, I was speaking in tongues when a woman there started shouting, "She's speaking Spanish! She's speaking Spanish!" Then she rushed over and stood in front of me and excitedly said, "You're speaking Spanish! I understand every word you're saying! You're praising God in Spanish!" It was a glorious experience that radically changed my life and opened up my prayer life to experiences I had never dreamed of. It will do the same for you as you *pray in tongues!*

Not everyone's experience is the same. In fact, Merlin Caruther's experience was quite different; he didn't feel anything. After he was prayed for, he received the baptism of the Holy Spirit by *faith*! I believe the Lord did it for me the way He did, so that when I told my father-in-law, a minister in the Church of Christ, about it, I could assure him I was speaking in a known, recognizable language that I don't know, and a woman there understood every word I was saying! Hallelujah!

As I have prayed with and ministered to many women through the years, I have come to believe that my Dad's love and *approval* set a foundation of trust and security in my life and make up. David praised God, *"But You are He who took me out of the womb, You have taught me to trust upon my mother's breast."* (Psalms 22: 9). Those first years of life are foundational, and I believe it was my Dad's love especially that has enabled me to have a close relationship with and love for Abba Daddy, our Heavenly Father. Mother loved us all too; she showed her love by cooking wonderful meals, doing mountains of laundry, and by spanking me and my brothers a lot. *"The rod and reproof give wisdom, but a child left to himself, brings shame to his mother."* (Proverbs 29:15). Mother was very kind and hospitable, but she made sure we kids knew right from wrong! She took us to church every Sunday morning, Sunday night, and Wednesday night. Daddy rarely spanked any of us, but when he did, it was memorable!

I had our last child, beautiful Christina, when I was 42. While she was 17, I started writing *Run To The Battle In Jesus' Name,* in December, 2004, and finished it in about eight months. My brother, Larry, and my pastor's wife, Sister Suzy of Church on the Rock in San Antonio, read the manuscript that fall and liked it. Sadly, Sister Suzy passed away the following year. Everyone else I offered it to for input was "too busy" or "didn't like to read." The Christian publishing houses I sent it to all returned it unread with brief notes saying they were "not accepting unsolicited manuscripts." Thus, except for two people, the book lay unread and dormant for almost three years; it was not yet God's time for it to be brought out.

In February, 2008, I prayed, "Lord, I am asking for at least *one* person, preferably a man, to read my book and say, 'Yes, this has value; this has worth; you should pursue getting it published,' or 'No, forget it.'" I felt a man would be more objective and give me a truer appraisal than a woman so I wanted a man's opinion.

In May that year I called a handyman, Thomas Magner, who had advertised in our Home Owners Association's newsletter, to do some work on our son Paul's investment property. On our second meeting, he told me, "I'm actually a Christian musician," and gave me a CD of five songs he had written and recorded. They are anointed, powerful songs. Thomas is a Catholic believer who received the baptism of the Holy Spirit during the Catholic charismatic movement in the 1980s.

I responded, "Well, I'm actually a Christian writer. Would you like to read the first five chapters of my book?" (It was usual to submit five chapters to a publisher so I had several sets.) He said yes, so I gave him the first five chapters.

He called the very *next day* and said he had read them! After nearly three years of no one expressing any interest in the book, a person had read five chapters in one day, and liked them! Stunned, I asked, "Would you like to read the rest of it?" Again, he said yes, and I gave him the rest of the manuscript. When he returned it, I found he had simply written in red ink across the top of some pages or occasionally at the end of a chapter, "Excellent." Praise the Lord!

Thomas was the answer to my prayer for "someone" (a man) to read my book. He made several suggestions that improved its structure. For the last two years, he has been urging me to complete *The Land of the Giants.* (I am busy with many things, go many places, and meet many people). I consider him a gifted friend and consulting editor. For these reasons, when he asked to write a Foreword for this book, I said yes.

May the book be a blessing and encouragement to you that God knows you, loves you and you were born for a purpose. God has given you an assignment, something you can do better (and probably differently) than anyone else on earth because you were designed for it, and it was designed for you! *"For we are His workmanship, created in Christ Jesus for good works, which God prepared beforehand that we should walk in them."* (Ephesians 2:10). The Lord has given you a talent, something that brings great satisfaction to you and is a blessing to others.

Do you have a dream in your heart? I believe every person has a God-given dream. If you don't know what yours is, pray about it. *"It is the glory of God to conceal a matter, but the glory of kings is to search out a matter."* (Proverbs 25:2). If you are a believer in the Lord Jesus, you are His child, and I believe He will lead you to it … and after step one, there will be step two, etc. Every step will be attained by faith, prayer, and following God's leading. The grace of our Lord Jesus Christ be with you, dear Reader. To God and Jesus Christ, His Son, be all glory and thanks!

"For as many as are led by the Spirit of God, these are sons of God" (Romans 8:14), and *"For I know the thoughts that I think toward you, says the Lord, thoughts of peace and not of evil, to give you a future and a hope. Then you will call upon me and I will listen to you."* (Jeremiah 29:11). Hallelujah!

Sincerely,
Donna Hamilton

The Vision

Write the vision and make it plain on tablets
That he may run who reads it.
— Habakkuk 2:2

In November, 1994, three friends and I had just returned from Washington D. C. from a prayer assignment to pray for God's Will to be done in the national elections. We returned with great joy at all the Lord revealed and did in our five days there. (The 104th Congress was elected two days after our return.) The following week while on my knees in my prayer closet, which was the laundry room in our townhouse, praying, praising, thanking God, and reading His word, a vivid, full-color vision unfolded before my eyes.

It began by my seeing myself in the armor of God. The Lord usually shows me myself the same way: dressed neck to foot in close-fitting, finely–linked mail armor, light and supple; a metal skull–cap type helmet on my head; a shield of faith, usually small and lightweight as it was this time (sometimes large and rectangular going down to my feet), secure on my left arm; and a big sword in my right hand which I wield very easily, lightly. "Supernaturally wielded" I once heard. The shoes vary; usually they are low cut, lightweight "dancing shoes," which is what they were this time, Sometimes there are little wings on the back, so that in the spirit I can go great distances fast, actually go in huge, leaping bounds that are close to flying, around the border of a state or large territory. Occasionally, but rarely, they are combat boots.

As the vision expanded, I saw that I was on a wide, brown plain, high–stepping, lifting my sword up and down as a majorette might do when leading a band; then I saw behind me two women dressed exactly like me. We were in perfect step. Behind them were three or four women, dressed in similar armor, with five or six women behind those, and as the vision enlarged, I saw row upon row of warrior women dressed in armor, marching together in perfect step, forming a huge triangle-shaped army!

Suddenly I was at the back, above the army, and saw women running in from every direction at the back, to join the army. They were dressed in a variety of ways. One large, big–boned woman was running in my direction. She looked like a pioneer woman: no make-up; gray hair in a bun; a big apron over her long skirt; and too–large, worn–looking men's boots with no laces were flopping on her feet. A black, cast-iron skillet was held high in her right hand.

I saw another woman up close, a young modern woman. She was wearing a sheath skirt and cardigan sweater. Her blonde hair was shoulder-–length in page–boy style. She was running so intently she was bent over, a rolling pin clutched in one hand. I saw then that all the women were carrying "weapons," a rake or hoe, one woman had a broom, another, a pitch fork. They were all running to become part of the army, rushing to get in the back row, and when it was full, another row would begin to form.

Later, as I thought about the vision, especially this part, I realized the women had only natural weapons; they didn't have spiritual weapons. In other words, they weren't equipped to fight spiritual battles. They didn't have the knowledge, understanding, or weapons to win against invisible enemies in the spirit realm. Remember Jesus said, "My people perish for lack of knowledge." (Hosea 4:6).

Then I saw one woman up close as she stepped into the back row. She was in regular street clothes, but as she put one foot forward, the armor of God was suddenly on her front half with her civilian clothes on behind! As she took another step forward, completing that step, suddenly she was fully clothed in the whole armor of God, including sword and shield, as were all the women ahead and beside her. She was part of the army now; her stride matching the others' perfectly.

As I looked at the rows, the women looked so strong. There was perfect order in the ranks; the rows were straight, the steps measured. The women were in unison; the army was one unit, marching as one force. It was beautiful.

The view shifted again, above the army and looking across the plain; it was obvious we were marching toward high hills far away to the right. Suddenly I was above the hills, looking down on a guard tower there; at its base stood a giant. He was looking out at the plain and I saw what he saw: a mighty triangle–shaped army, growing larger by the moment, was moving across the plain towards the hill where he was. The army was marching in such unity and power that the ground shook slightly with every step. It seemed I could hear a song then, coming faintly across the plain; the army was singing!

The giant began to tremble. Now I saw there was a second giant behind him, down below at the foot of the hill. I knew he was there to get a watchman's report. The ground shook a little harder with every step as the army advanced, and with fear the first giant called out to the one below, "The women are coming! The women are coming!"

And I knew they were coming to get back what Satan had stolen from them. This was an army of the Lord's women, dressed in the whole armor of God and carrying mighty weapons of warfare, marching with power and purpose to The Land of the Giants.

The title of this book is based on that vision. By sharing it, I hope to stir in you a desire to be a warrior woman, dressed and equipped with the whole armor of God, part of the army of the Lord!

The vision ended there that day. A second vision came a few days later while I was on my knees in the same place, praying. It picked up where the first one ended, but it's not to share right now. The meaning of the first vision was clear; I would be leading an army of spiritually awakened, informed, and armed women someday—to fight the devil and his evil hordes and recover what had been stolen from them.

As I pondered this vision and its implications, I wondered how the Lord would do this. "No one knows me, Lord, except my friends and a few others. How could I lead an army of women and teach them about spiritual warfare?" I asked the Lord this question. He didn't answer, but I am used to that and actually not bothered by it. I know He will answer or show me in His time, which generally is when I need to know it!

I now believe this teaching on prayer and spiritual warfare will initially and perhaps primarily be through writing books in which I share, with scriptures, various adventures and experiences God has given me; as well as

His wonderful, awesome answers to prayer and the things He taught me through them. Hopefully, my mistakes and errors, as well as victories, will help others avoid those same pitfalls and win their own battles. *"Listen to counsel and receive instruction, that you may be wise in your latter days."* (Proverbs 19:20).

In the vision, I didn't seem particularly aware of the women behind me, except for the few near me, and that makes sense if I am teaching through books. Women whom I may never have the joy of meeting here on earth, nevertheless, can learn what God has taught me by reading about my experiences. I've learned many valuable truths from those of past generations by reading accounts of their experiences—and will share a couple of those in this book.

"One generation shall praise Your works to another, and shall tell Your mighty acts." (Psalms 145:4). "May it be so with me, Lord, and may I also teach Your women to fight their battles with faith, words (both Yours and theirs), the blood of Jesus, and the full armor of God! In Jesus' Name I ask this! Amen." Hallelujah!

"When a strong man, fully armed, guards his own palace, his goods are in peace. But when a stronger than he comes upon him and overcomes him, he takes from him all his armor in which he trusted, and divides his spoils." (Luke 11:21–22), and "You are of God, little children, and have overcome them, because He who is in you is greater than he who is in the world." **(1 John 4:4)! "Yes, Lord!" and Praise the Lord!**

Chapter 1

I Have an Eight to Twelve–Page Paper Due Tomorrow

If any of you lacks wisdom, let him ask of God,
who gives to all liberally, And without reproach,
and it will be given to him
— James 1:5–6a

"Mom, I called to ask you for prayer. I have an eight to twelve–page paper due tomorrow, and I haven't even decided what to write about." One day in the spring of 2006, I answered the phone and heard these words from our son, Torrey, who was a "firstie" (*senior*) at the United states Air Force Academy in Colorado Springs, Colorado.

He went on to explain, "We got the assignment three weeks ago, but it's finals week and I've had so much to do preparing for finals with my other classes and leadership duties, I haven't even decided on a subject yet."

"What is the actual assignment?" I asked.

"We're supposed to write about cooperation between two branches of the services, citing a specific example with research on its development, history, implementation, effects, and current status. The paper's supposed to be between eight and twelve pages." (I knew this meant typed pages.)

"So it could be about the Air Force cooperating with the Army, Navy, or Coast Guard?" I asked.

"Yes."

"Well, son, let's ask the Lord what you should write about. Let's pray in tongues about it, okay?" was my response.

"Okay," he said, and we both started quietly praying in our prayer languages. The apostle Paul wrote in 1 Corinthians 14:15, *"I will pray with the spirit and I will pray with the understanding also."*

So after praying in the spirit a few moments, I prayed in English. "Heavenly Father, You know all this. You know all Torrey's responsibilities, being a Team Leader supervising the "doolies" (*freshmen*) that have been assigned to him to guide and train. You know all his Bible study, the finals, physical duties, etc., and so, Abba Daddy, we are asking you now to show us specifically what he should write about on cooperation between two branches of the military."

All this time, Torrey was quietly praying in his prayer language, agreeing with me in my prayer. The word of God tells us in Matthew 18:19, *"Again, I say to you that if two of you agree on earth concerning anything that they ask, it will be done for them by My Father in heaven."* Jesus Himself said this. I reminded the Lord of this scripture and thanked Him that He would guide us in this.

As I resumed praying in the spirit (praying in tongues), in a few moments I "saw" the ocean. Sunlight was sparkling on water all around. My view was just above the water, looking across a wide expanse of sea with sunlight dancing on the surface. Then far off to my right, I "saw" a ship, and suddenly up close, I looked up and saw the silhouettes of what looked like the tails of small airplanes sticking out above the side of the ship. There were four or five of them in a row just jutting out over the side of the ship.

A thought came to me as I remembered an old black–and–white movie I once saw on television about General Doolittle's training a handful of pilots to take off in their planes from the deck of ships in World War II. It was amazing; an innovative and risky undertaking that helped turned the tide of the war.

"Torrey, does the Air Force still fly planes off the decks of Navy ships?"

"Yes, Mom!" he immediately replied. "That's what my roommate suggested two weeks ago, but I haven't even had time to think about it."

I described to him the picture the Lord had just shown me. We both knew then this was his subject. The word tells us, *"In the mouth of two or three witnesses, every word will be confirmed."* (2 Corinthians 13:1), and this picture or "vision" confirmed what his roommate had suggested—no doubt by the Lord's leading, though he might not have realized it.

I asked the Lord to guide Torrey in his research, give him wisdom, and inspire the words he wrote because Proverbs 16:1 says, *"A man may order (organize) his thoughts, but the Lord inspires the words he says."* And finally I asked the Lord to help him make it "a paper of excellence," that he would "get an 'A' on it, in Jesus' Name." Hallelujah!

We hung up quickly when Torrey told me the paper was due by midnight the next night, Thursday. It was

Wednesday noon when he called, so he had 36 hours from research to writing and turning it in! That included getting some sleep and one other class the next afternoon.

My dad, who lived with us then (now gone to heaven), invited me out to lunch. I was in high spirits as we went, praising the Lord over this wonderful answer to prayer.

Later as we were leaving the restaurant, I struck up a conversation with an older lady, and as usual, the conversation turned to the Lord. I shared with her what had happened over the phone with our son and told her about the vision the Lord had given. I also told her about my prayer that Torrey would get an 'A' on the paper.

She looked up at me, lifted one finger, and with a smile and a twinkle in her eye, said, "And I pray that he will get an 'A plus!'"

Wow, that was kind of stretching it for me. I had thought an 'A' would be awesome and at the United States Air Force Academy especially, it is. To ask for an 'A plus' seemed, well, almost unreasonable. "O, ye of little faith!" Jesus said several times to His disciples.

Well, Friday afternoon Torrey called and said excitedly, "Mom, I turned in my paper on time—and I got an 'A plus!'" Praise the Lord! God is so good.

A few days ago, I phoned Torrey and told him I'd like to include this incident in the book and asked "Do you remember it?"

"I remember it very well," was his instant reply. "I still have the paper in my files. My professor was enthusiastic about it and made some nice comments about it to the class." Thank you again, Lord!

My point in telling you this is to stir you up to pray about everything—big and small, emotional, physical, financial, and spiritual. *"God is our refuge and strength; a very present help in time of trouble."* (Psalms 46:1). He has all the answers. He knows everything. He knows what we should do in every circumstance and He is willing, wanting, and waiting to help you if you will just **ask**.

"Now to Him who is able to do exceedingly abundantly above all that we ask or think, according to the power that works in us, to Him be glory in the church by Christ Jesus throughout all ages, world without end. Amen." **(Ephesians 3:20)**

Chapter 2

Daddy, That Boy is in the Pool with His Clothes On

Behold, an angel of the Lord appeared to Joseph in a dream, saying, "Arise, take the young Child and His mother, flee to Egypt, And stay there until I bring you word, for Herod will seek the young Child to destroy Him."
— Matthew 2:13

When our daughter Deborah and James, her boyfriend, became engaged; we had an engagement party in their honor. With James' family, our family, and friends, perhaps forty people were at our home that beautiful, balmy Saturday afternoon in April, 1986.

We were leasing a two–story home with a beautiful pool in the over-sized backyard. Our younger son, Torrey, was only two years old when we moved in. Concerned for his safety, after we moved in, I went to the backyard, stood at one end of the pool and prayed over it.

With one hand stretched towards the pool, I rebuked, "Any spirit of death that might be over the pool," and commanded it, "in Jesus' name, depart and never return!"

I also prayed, "Lord, I ask that there *never* be a death in this pool—that You will set an angel here, so that if anyone should ever fall in or be in trouble, someone will see and help him, in **Jesus'** Name! Thank You!" Months had passed since then.

One young mom had come to the party with several of James' friends, her five–year old son with her. I cautioned her to please keep a close watch on him around the pool. Every time I noticed, she had him near her.

At a certain point, I asked everyone to come inside while James and Deborah cut their engagement cake. After people were served, I took a piece of cake, went into the living room, and sat in a folding chair beside Ed who was eating cake and talking to a man on the other side of him.

All at once, Torrey, who was barely *three years old* (if even that because his birthday is *in* April), walked up to Ed, stood right in front of him and said, "Daddy, that boy's in the pool with his clothes on." Ed reacted quicker than anyone I've ever seen. He jumped to his feet in one motion, cake, plate, and fork flying from his hands and **ran** out onto the patio. The man followed, and I was behind him. The little boy was face down *under the water* in the shallow end of the pool, the end farthest from the patio doors.

Ed ran along the side, jumped into the pool, pushed over to him against chest–high water, and put his face and head *under wate*r to reach him on the bottom of the pool. He scooped him up holding him close, carried him up the steps of the pool, and laid him face down on the grass. One of the guests rushed over, identified himself as a paramedic, and dropped to his knees beside Ed and the little boy.

By this time, others were streaming out of the house to see what was going on. The young mother was hysterical, crying and screaming, "I was just with him two minutes ago! He was just with me!"

I was praying in tongues quietly, but earnestly. Others were praying too; I could hear them as the two men bent over him. The paramedic or Ed pushed on his stomach and he began to cough and sputter, spit up some water, and started to cry. He was dazed and bewildered, but, praise God, he was all right!

Well, after things had settled down, and I had cleaned up the cake and frosting from the carpet; I noticed one of James' friends, a young man in his early twenties who was upset. In fact, he was distraught.

Finally, I approached him as he was standing off alone and gently asked, "Are you all right?"

"No," he said, shaking his head, "about two weeks ago I had a dream about 'Joey' (*not the little boy's real name, I don't remember it*). He was in water and was drowning. His mom was in the dream, but she had turned away; her back was to him and she didn't know he was in trouble. I woke up with a start and a strong sense that he was in danger of this, and God wanted me to warn his mom to really guard him when he was around water. I kept feeling I should tell her about my dream and warn her, but I didn't. I was afraid she'd think I was weird or crazy or strange, so I didn't. Over and over, I wanted tell her, but didn't."

Close to tears, he burst out, "He almost drowned today! He could have died, and it's *my* fault. I never told her!"

As he was speaking, I was quietly praying in tongues asking God for wisdom and insight. I believe some understanding was given to me.

First of all, I told him about my prayer over the pool— that there would **never** be a death in that pool! I pointed out to him that God is faithful and had used a *three–year–old,* our son, to tell my husband about Joey's being in the pool. Thank you, Jesus! He was listening intently.

About the dream, I said, "Yes, you were supposed to warn her, but God knew this is new to you. You didn't understand things like this, and you talked yourself out of telling her about the dream, but God in His mercy had a back–up plan."

"Now this is the good news," I told him. "We know that *'all things work together for good to those who love God, to those who are the called according to His purpose.'* (Romans 8:28). You love Him and you are called. Every believer is. God is using this to help you grow. I believe God is going to use you prophetically more and more. You probably will have more dreams or 'words' for people, and this is the thing about it, from now on you *will* tell people the things God shows you. You will not be afraid or hold back about it again. God has let you see today how *vital* it is to do what He tells you. It could be a matter of life or death for someone—and from now on, you *will* obey the Lord!"

He seemed comforted and encouraged by my words. Then we prayed together and asked God to forgive him, we *thanked* Him for protecting Joey, and he told God that in the future he would trust Him and do what he felt He wanted him to do.

Also, I told him he needed to forgive *himself* too and "move on." We have all failed or disobeyed God for "whatever" reasons. *"For all have sinned and fall short of the glory of God."* (Romans 3:23). This is why we all need to receive Jesus into our heart. God forgives *us* because of *His* obedience and sacrifice, when we ask Him to be our Savior.

Now I want to encourage *you*, dear Reader; if you failed to do something God told or led you to do, and which of us hasn't; and have not made it right with Him, please ask Him to forgive you. Make up your mind that next time, with His help, you will do as He says. God knows you; He loves you, and He is very patient with us. He will forgive you if you ask and will give you another chance, another opportunity, to be a part of His plan for someone else, and this will be a blessing in your life.

Remember, if we don't fulfill God's assignments or purpose, it affects other people. Some things will affect *many* people.

I believe God had great mercy on the young man (and all of us!) at the party because he was young in the Lord and unfamiliar with things such as a warning in a dream; though there are numerous examples of this in the Bible. I also believe the Holy Spirit had led me to pray over the pool; this gave God something to work with to save Joey.

Prayer changes things. When we pray, we invite God into our circumstances; and it makes all the difference.

Regarding the young man not recognizing it was a dream from God, at least not well enough to share it, remember the story of Samuel in the Bible.

When Samuel, who later became a mighty prophet of God, was a child, it happened one night *"that while Samuel was lying down to sleep, that the Lord called Samuel. And he answered, 'Here I am!' So he ran to Eli (the priest) and said, 'Here I am, for you called me.'*

"And he said, 'I did not call; lie down again.' And he went and lay down.

"And the Lord called yet again, 'Samuel!'

"So Samuel arose and went to Eli, and said, 'Here I am, for you called me.'

"And he answered, 'I did not call, my son; lie down again.' (Now Samuel did not yet know the Lord, nor was the word of the Lord yet revealed to him.)

"And the Lord called Samuel again the third time. Then he arose and went to Eli, and said, 'Here I am, for you did call me.'

"Then Eli perceived that the Lord had called the boy. Therefore Eli said to Samuel, 'Go, lie down; and it shall be, if He calls you, that you must say, "Speak, Lord, for your servant hears."'

"So Samuel went and lay down in his place. Then the Lord came and stood and called as at other times, 'Samuel! Samuel!'

"And Samuel answered, 'Speak, for Your servant hears.'

"Then the Lord said to Samuel, 'Behold, I will do something in Israel at which both ears of everyone who hears it will tingle...'" You can read this whole account in 1 Samuel 3:3–11.

See how gracious and patient God is with us.

Jesus said, *"To whom much is given, much will be required; and to whom much has been committed, of him they will ask the more."* (Luke 12:48), so I believe the converse is also true—to whom little is given, little will be required; to whom little has been committed, of him they will ask the less.

As we grow in the Lord, He can trust us with more and also requires more of us in obedience. It is just as we do with our children; we expect "more," better behavior for example, from an adult child than a toddler. This doesn't mean God loves the mature believer more than the baby—no. He loves us all "to the **max**," but He will use a mature believer sometimes in ways He won't use a new believer. God is so good; He teaches us things through our mistakes too, as well as our "successes."

There is a sequel to this pool event, however.

I told several close friends (women who pray) what had happened with the little boy at the engagement party. The word says, *"Then those who feared the Lord spoke to one another, and the Lord listened and heard them."* (Malachi 3:16). This included, of course, telling them about my earlier prayer over the pool. We praised and thanked God for His grace to everyone involved.

Well, the following week, one of those friends called and told me she had shared my story with another friend of hers and added, "My friend would like you to come anoint their house and pray over their pool."

They had just recently moved into a house with an unfenced pool, had three young children, plus she babysat two nieces and a nephew five days a week; so she had *six* young children on the weekdays (two or three were in school part of the day), and their own children all the time. They didn't have money to fence the pool right then. She was in constant fear that one of the children would get out of the house into the back yard, and fall into the pool. In addition to this, she didn't know how to swim!

I told my friend, "Yes, I will go."

A few days later on a rather overcast day, we went to her friend's home. Her friend, who was Hispanic, didn't speak English, so she and I couldn't really communicate, except through our mutual friend and gestures.

We anointed the house, which was full of children including a toddler; then they took me to the backyard. I could see why she was so concerned. The edge of that pool was only 5 or 6 feet from the sliding patio door. It filled the yard except for one small area.

I prayed a very similar prayer to the one I had prayed over our own pool, rebuking a spirit of death and asking the Lord to set an angel there to guard, and even be *in* the pool, if anyone ever fell in or was drowning. I prayed that the angel would push them up to the surface and that there would "*never be a death* in that pool—in Jesus' name!"

The woman hugged me tightly before we left. I asked my friend to tell her what I had been saying while praying.

Well, less than two weeks later, my friend called to tell me what had happened. Somehow some of the children got out of the house into the backyard. When her friend saw it, she rushed out to get them. The toddler was right at the edge of the pool, and to her horror, as she was hurrying to him, he lost his balance and fell in!

She rushed to the side and got on her knees reaching out for him. He was under the water out of her reach. "Then," she said, "the baby just shot out of the water right towards her, into her arms; she grabbed him and lifted him out!" Praise the Lord!

You know, when I think of this incident happening so closely upon the heels of the other, I truly thank God for His orchestration of these events. If the incident hadn't happened with Joey, I wouldn't have shared that praise report with my friend, and she wouldn't have told her other friend about it; the pool might not have been prayed over; an angel might not have been assigned there, etc.

Some might say it was just a coincidence the baby shot up into her arms, but I believe God had an angel push or lift him to the surface, and what better place than into his mother's arms? There is also the fact that she arrived *just in time* to see him fall in! A few seconds could have changed everything. (Probably the angel told her to go check on the children "Now!") I give God the glory for all these things.

"When you pray, something happens that would not have happened if you had not prayed." Isn't that beautiful? A great man of God, Mike Murdock, said that. But long before that, JESUS said, *"If you abide in Me and My words abide in you, you will ask what you desire, and it shall be done for you."* (John 15:7). Hallelujah! Thank you, Lord.

***"Yes, we had the sentence of death in ourselves, that we should not trust in ourselves, but in God who raises the dead, who delivered us from so great a death ...in whom we trust that He will still deliver us, you also helping together in prayer for us..."* (2 Corinthians 1:9–11) Dear Reader, please pray for those around you!**

CHAPTER 3

IT HAPPENED AT THE BEACH

"Do you not say, 'There are still four months and then comes the harvest?' Behold, I say to you, lift up your eyes and look at the fields, For they are already white for harvest!"
— John 4:35

About obeying the Lord, when it is something you might not naturally do, it is important to understand that the Lord always has a reason, a purpose, when He asks us to do something. Here is an example.

While some of our children were still at home, we had a membership at Mountain Lakes, a beautiful campground near Lytle Creek, California. The builders had brought in sand to create a beach along a roped–off section of the lake.

One weekend while we were there, I was in my swimsuit sitting on a towel on the beach, reading and enjoying the sunshine while the rest of the family were off doing other things. A group of eight or nine young people came to the quiet area where I was, put down their towels, cooler, etc., turned on a boom box, and started playing around. Some ran into the water where the young men were catching the girls and throwing them into deeper water; others were tossing a Frisbee.

I was sitting there watching, quietly praying for them both in tongues and English, that they would come to know the Lord and each would fulfill God's purpose for his or her life. Suddenly, the thought came into my heart that I should speak to them about the Lord!

As I continued praying, the thought grew clearer, and my heart beat faster. I was somewhat intimidated to approach them, but reasoned, "*Well, the worst they can do is tell me no. I don't think they'll get violent or start swearing or anything.*" I also realized this was the only time in all of history we would all be together on this earth. I thought, "*I'll probably never see any of them again, so I might as well do it.*" That is not the best reason to obey the Lord, but at the time it bolstered my courage.

After prayer I decided to just ask if I could speak to them; so I stood up, tied the towel around my waist, walked to the nearest young man and loudly asked, "Uh, could I say something to all of you please?"

I had to repeat my request because of the loud music, but once he understood what I wanted, he reached back and down, turned off the boom box, and the music suddenly stopped. Some of them looked over at us, and he called out, "This lady wants to say something to us. Hey, she wants to say something!"

Would you believe the ones in the water came out of the water, and the ones horsing around on the sand came over, and they all stood more or less in a semi–circle in front of me, looking at me expectantly to see what this lady had to say! Praise God, I had prayed before standing up, asking the Lord to guide me in what to say and to open their hearts to His message.

"Thank you for letting me speak to you. As I was sitting there watching you, I felt the Lord loves you very much, each one of you, and He wanted me to tell you that. And He has a plan for each of your lives; something He created you to do." They sat down on the sand.

"I was wondering, do you understand about the world, that God created it? He made it beautiful, perfect, and He gave it to the man He had created, Adam, and his wife, Eve. God gave Adam everything and told him there was only one thing he couldn't do, and that was to eat of the Tree of the Knowledge of Good and Evil. He was forbidden to eat its fruit.

"But the devil, who used to be an angel, had rebelled against God and been thrown out of heaven. He hated God and was jealous that He had given this beautiful earth to man. He despised Adam and Eve; he wanted the earth for himself. He knew the only way he could get it was to make Adam and Eve sin or disobey God. He set out to do this, watched for his chance, and lured Eve into eating the fruit. Then she took some and gave it to Adam. That is how sin, which is disobedience to God, entered the world. But God knew this would happen before He created Adam."

Briefly in about three or four minutes I explained about God's choosing Abraham to start a people through whom He would send the Savior, Jesus the Son of God, who became the sacrifice for our sins, so that we could have peace with God. I shared that when we receive Jesus as Lord and Savior, God counts the Lord's death as payment for *our* sins and attributes or "credits" *His* righteousness and obedience to us. *"He was wounded for our transgressions and was bruised for our iniquities; the chastisement (punishment) for our peace was upon Him, and by His stripes we are healed."* (Isaiah 53:5).

Then I asked if any of them would like to receive Jesus as his or her Savior that day. One girl said, "I am a Christian," and one young man said, "I go to church every week," and then one or two others went back to the water. Several remained and I asked the question again. I think three of the young men and a girl raised their hands. I led them in prayer to receive Jesus as Lord and to give their lives to Him. Then I asked, "Is this the first time you've asked the Lord into your heart?" and one young man raised his hand. Hallelujah!

I prayed for them, asking God to bless them, to send other believers into their lives, and to lead them each to a good home church (that means a church that would be their spiritual home), with pastors who would love them and teach them about the Lord.

Dear Reader, I am very glad I obeyed the Lord that day. Jesus said, *"Behold, I stand at the door and knock. If any man hears My voice and opens the door, I will come in to him and dine with him and he with Me."* (Revelation 3:20). He was speaking of the "door" of a person's heart. He knew their hearts, that one was ready to receive Him as Lord and Savior and others would recommit their lives to Him.

If I had refused to speak to them, the Lord would have had to set up another circumstance and call someone else to do it. Who knows when another opportunity would have come for them individually or as a group?

Kathryn Kulhman had a powerful, international healing ministry. She said the Lord called two men before her, but they both refused. They did not want the criticism and opposition that comes with a healing ministry. Satan hates healing because people see the *power* and the *love of God* when people are visibly healed, and many come to the Lord because of it. They were not willing to pay the price for God's call; she was the third one. Hundreds of thousands of people received the Lord in her meetings and thousands were healed. I thank God for her.

Those two men remind me of what is written about many rulers back in the time Jesus walked on the earth. *"Nevertheless even among the rulers many believed in Him, but because of the Pharisees they did not confess Him, lest they should be put out of the synagogue; for they loved the praise of men more than the praise of God."* (John 12:42–43).

Dear Reader, please determine that you will follow Jesus all the way, that you will love the praise of God more than the praise of men. That, as the apostle Paul did, you will *"press toward the goal for the prize of the high calling of God in Christ Jesus."* (Philippians 3:14). The high calling of God will be different for each of us. Some may have similar calls, but no two are exactly the same. Trust Him. *Jesus knows us better than we know ourselves,* and He knows the purpose for which He created each of us. *"All things were made through Him, and without Him nothing was made that was made."* (John 1:3).

Be assured when the Lord gives you a task, it's important. *"It is the glory of God to conceal a matter, but the glory of kings is to search out a matter."* (Proverbs 25:2). At a future point, you might also learn that what you did was *one step* in a much larger, magnificent endeavor and that will bring you additional joy. But in any case, you obeyed the Lord! Remember—*"The end of a thing is better than its beginning, and the patient in spirit is better than the proud in spirit."* (Ecclesiastes 7:8). This means it's easier to start something, than it is to finish it. Even though a person who is proud in spirit might boast of the great things he is *going* to do, it is better for someone patient in spirit to steadily plod along and complete what he has started!

"How then shall they call on Him in whom they have not believed? And how shall they believe in Him of whom they have not heard? And how shall they hear without a preacher? And how shall they preach unless they are sent? As it is written: 'How beautiful are the feet of those who preach the gospel of peace, who bring glad tidings of good things!'" **(Romans 10:14–15). Sometimes, dear Reader, you will be the one who is sent.**

Chapter 4

They're Going to Remove Part of His Brain

If the whole body were an eye, where would be the hearing? If the whole body were hearing, where would be the smelling? But now God has set the members, each one of them, in the body just as He pleased.
— 1 Corinthians 12:17–18

Sometimes when praying, ideas or words or even pictures come to me. I measure them against the word of God to see if they are in line with His revealed will, and if I don't feel a check or "stop" in my spirit, I go ahead and ask or pray for whatever it is that came into my heart. I believe this is one aspect (part) of being "led by the Spirit." Here is an example.

Recently in our adult Sunday morning Bible class, a prayer request was shared by a certain woman. She said the week before she had felt led to call a friend, a former school mate she hadn't talked to in a long time.

She said, "He told me their little twenty-two-month old son is going to have brain surgery next week. A part of his brain is 'like a lump;' all the nerves are mashed together. He has seizures and can't walk or talk, so they're going to remove part of his brain, a piece about the size of a quarter next week. They hope that will help him."

When she said that, out of all the prayer requests that day that one came into my spirit and *lodged* there. I couldn't get away from it. My heart was horrified to think that a piece of that baby's *brain* "about the size of a quarter" was going to be removed! While others were sharing their praise reports or prayer requests, I started quietly praying in tongues about this, and after a few minutes, the word "Disentangled" came into my spirit. I had such a desire to speak to that little one's brain and *command* those nerves to "Separate and be *disentangled*—in JESUS' Name!"

With so many prayer requests that day, there was no opportunity during our group prayer to do this; plus I had a strong check (STOP) in my spirit about praying in this large group of men and women as forcefully as I wanted.

We need to use wisdom about things like this; we do not want to offend others with our actions. The apostle Paul said, *"To the weak I became as weak... I have become all things to all men that I might by all means save some."* (I Corinthians 9:22). In other words, consider other people before you jump in.

He gives several examples of how we need to love one another and allow each person liberty in his faith walk with God and not offend someone who might misunderstand our own faith walk with the Lord.

One example Paul gave was, *"For one believes he may eat all things, but he who is weak eats only vegetables. Let not him who eats despise him who does not eat, and let not him who does not eat judge him who eats, for God has received him."* (Romans 14:2–3). In other words, God accepts each person "where he is" in his beliefs as long as he believes in and belongs to JESUS. In His own time and way, God will gradually teach us the best ways—His ways, as we grow in the grace and knowledge of the Lord.

Paul sums it up so beautifully, *"Who are you to judge another man's servant? To his own master he stands or falls. Indeed, he will be made to stand, for God is able to make him stand... for if we live, we live to the Lord; and if we die, we die to the Lord. Therefore, whether we live or die, we are the Lord's."* (Romans 14:4,8). Hallelujah!

This is showing us we are not to judge one another; even though we are different, but rather accept one another with love. If we have a feeling something is going to offend someone else, unless the Lord specifically leads us to do or say it (and in that case, just obey Him and leave the results to Him), let us *walk in love,* wisdom, and self control (or restraint) and not do it. I felt I should wait to pray about this matter privately, so that's what I did.

After class, I sought out the young woman and shared with her my strong desire to pray for the little boy, whom I'll call Matthew. We went to some chairs on one side of the room, sat down, joined hands, and PRAYED. I felt such sorrow for the parents and compassion for little Matthew that I was close to tears as I prayed for mercy for them and healing for Matthew.

Of course, I prayed in tongues part of the time and as I did, I "saw" what I believe was the area of his brain where the nerves were "in a lump," squeezed or melded into an indistinguishable mass. A few single nerves were coming out at the top, but the body of it was a small, messy lump. I believe this picture was a word of knowledge, one of the nine gifts of the Holy Spirit. (I Corinthians 12:7-8).

"In Jesus' Name," I commanded those nerves, "separate and be *disentangled*! And nerves, each of you become strengthened, whole, and distinct, in JESUS' name!" We prayed some other things about it too.

Well, the next Sunday, she reported that Matthew was doing better and a week later, she announced to the class that when the doctors did the surgery they "*didn't have to remove any of his brain*! They just separated some of the nerves in a tiny little spot but didn't remove anything. Matthew is doing great!" (Thank You, Jesus!) After class she told me, "They just *untangled* some of the nerves." That sounds a lot like "disentangled" to me; praise God. To God be the glory!

I only tell you this to show you that *not everything is everyone's job*. Different people have different gifts and assignments. For me, the only real "prayer burden" I received that day in class was for little Matthew. I like to think other people received their own "burden" over other prayer requests. We cannot bear the burdens of the whole world; only Jesus can, and He *did* when He died on the cross.

One of Satan's favorite ploys is to make someone feel he or she is not doing his duty if he doesn't participate in every activity. God does not overload people; usually we do that to ourselves or others. It all goes back to the cross though and what Jesus did there, for that is where we come into unity or agreement (partnership) with God in His plans for us.

In Ephesians 4:14–16, we are told *"That we should no longer be children, tossed to and fro and carried about with every wind of doctrine... but, speaking the truth in love, may grow up in all things into Him who is the head—Christ—from whom the whole body, joined and knit together by what every joint supplies, … by which every part does its share, causes growth of the body...in love."*

This is part of what the apostle Paul meant when he wrote: *"Now there are diversities of gifts, but the same Spirit. There are differences of ministries, but the same Lord. And there are diversities of activities, but it is the same God who works all in all."* (I Corinthians 12:4–6). Isn't that beautiful?

As you continue to love God, He will guide you into His "good, acceptable, and perfect will" for you (Romans 12:2). These three "levels" or aspects of God's will are perhaps degrees of our walking in or into His *ultimate* plan for each of us. In other words, as we grow in the Lord and are obedient to Him, He increasingly leads us forward more and more into the *fullness* of His plan for our individual lives and ministries. Every person has a gift or talent, a special ability given by God—and usually more than one. (Hospitality is a beautiful gift.) Know that He will give you opportunities to minister in your anointing (to use your gifts) if you desire it and ask Him, because it is *His will* for you to use them. Be of good cheer; God loves you. He is for you.

"Therefore, my beloved, as you have always obeyed, not as in my presence only, but much more in my absence, work out your own salvation with fear and trembling: for it is God who works in you both to will (desire) and to do (take action) for His good pleasure." **(Philippians 2:12–13). Hallelujah!**

Chapter 5

My Husband Hasn't Been to Church for 23 Years

"For I have not spoken on My own authority, but the Father Who sent Me Gave me a command, what I should say and what I should speak."
— John 14:49

I want to encourage you to trust the Holy Spirit when you pray even if it seems different than what you have seen others do or have done yourself. I believe we can trust Heavenly Father to lead us just as He led Jesus and to show us "what we should say and what we should speak." Trust the Holy One. *"But you have an anointing from the Holy One and you know all things."* (I John 2:20.) Here is an example from my own experience. It happened in our home church in southern California.

One Sunday morning after church as people were leaving, I noticed a well–dressed older woman sitting quietly at the end of a pew wiping her eyes; it was obvious she had been crying. I was drawn to her, greeted her softly, introduced myself, and asked if there was "anything I could do to help? Could I pray with her about anything?"

She said, "My husband hasn't been to church for 23 years. He received the Lord years ago but got hurt over something that happened and has never been back to church since." She said it "hurt her so much every Sunday to leave him sitting in his easy chair reading the Sunday paper when she left for church." Her heart was aching over this, plus she was concerned about his salvation. She told me his name; I'll call him Bill Taylor.

I asked if she would like me to pray with her about it—that we would "agree" together (Matthew 18:19) that he would come back to church, and she consented. Since we were in a church setting where praying in tongues was taught and practiced, I prayed both in English and tongues about this.

After a little while, words and scriptures came up forcefully, and I heard myself **strongly** saying, "Bill Taylor, I speak to you in the name of JESUS CHRIST, your Lord and Savior, to come back into fellowship with His church! We break 'every high thing that exalts itself against the knowledge of God,' every spirit of accusation and separation from God, and in Jesus' name, I speak to your *spirit*. Get up from your easy chair, and REPORT FOR DUTY!

"You have a divine calling and God created you for His purpose, and you shall NOT BE AWOL any longer! Get back to the Lord and Savior of your soul! We call you back to Him, to Active Duty, serving Him and doing what He has created you for! In JESUS' name, we agree on this according to God's word—*'If two of you agree on earth as touching any matter, it shall be done for them by My Father in heaven!'"* (Matthew18:19).

Almost as I was speaking these words to his spirit, on another level my mind was saying, "Can I do this, Lord? Is this allowed?" but it was so strong in me and so forceful that I dared not stop. The prayer covered more than what is recorded here—that he would *forgive* whoever or whatever had hurt him so long ago, but this was the heart of it.

I have been led to pray this way only once or twice since then (speaking to someone's spirit). Actually, I believe it is prophesying more than "praying." It is as though one *knows* the will of God for the situation and declares it more than "requests" it.

Anyway, he was at church with her the *following Sunday!* She told me later that when she got home after we prayed that day, he was restless then agitated, and by Tuesday he told her he wanted to start going to church again! Praise the Lord! The LORD did it.

They came to the same home Bible study or "cell group" that we did just a week or two later. She introduced us, and when she told him I was "the one who had prayed with her for him to come back to church," at that first meeting, Bill shared the following with me privately.

"When I was young, I worked in a factory with an older man who was a Christian. I wasn't, and I harassed him all the time. Our work stations were next to each other, and I belittled and swore at him every day. We both brought our lunch boxes and ate together, and he would read the Bible every noon. I could hardly stand it. I had a chip on my shoulder towards him and found fault with him over anything I could.

"For twelve years this went on. He never gave up on me but kept talking to me about God and praying for me. I started listening, though I didn't tell him, and finally, one day I gave my heart to the Lord.

"He started teaching me the Bible; we had a Bible study at lunch then. For twelve days we did this. We were both so happy that I had received the Lord! We laughed and talked, and he was teaching me so much. Then one day he had an errand to do at noon, so he told me goodbye with a big smile. I was waiting for him to come back after lunch, but he didn't come back. That wasn't like him to be late.

"Finally someone from the front office came back and told me they had received a phone call from the police. While crossing a street, he had been hit by a car. He was dead." Tears filled his eyes as he told me this.

"Why?" he asked. "Why did God let that happen? I berated him for twelve years while he prayed for me; then we had twelve days together after I became a Christian. I was so angry with God that I stopped going to church and hadn't been back all these years. Why did God let that happen?"

As he was talking, I was praying for wisdom, asking God what to say to him. When he ended, this thought came to me, "Instead of being mad at God for taking him right then, did you ever *thank* God for the twelve days you had with him? Did you ever think that maybe his time to go was earlier than that, and maybe God in His goodness, let your friend live to see you be saved and then let him have twelve wonderful days of fellowship with you?

"He had prayed for you for twelve years, and God let him see the answer to his prayers for twelve days; a day for each year he'd prayed for you. Maybe his time to go had been the year before, or six months before, or two weeks before, but God gave him that gift, and gave you that gift too. Have you ever thanked God for the twelve days you had together as Christian brothers?"

With tears in his eyes, he shook his head and said, "No."

With tears in my eyes, I said, "Why don't we thank Him together?" We clasped hands, bowed our heads and prayed together.

I believe the Lord healed the hurt in his heart that night. He became a faithful, regular member and participant in church activities, a faithful servant of the Lord with a smile on his face and a twinkle in his eye. I thank God for the privilege of knowing "Bill Taylor," a fine Christian man. But the point of my writing this is that the Lord led me to pray in a new way that morning, and I heard statements coming out of my mouth that I had never thought of before—speaking to someone's spirit. As stated, I believe this is more prophesying than praying.

Maybe somehow, by the Spirit of the Lord, I was speaking directly to Bill Taylor's spirit; the Lord knows. It was not "my" prayer, believe me; those thoughts had never entered my mind. Those thoughts came into my *spirit* that day. It was precious Holy Spirit praying through me, *the will of the Father* with power and faith. The Word of God tells us "the anointing breaks the yoke." (Isaiah 10:27), and precious Holy Spirit had anointed me to pray an anointed prayer from God's throne, I believe, not from my mind or thoughts.

I cannot emphasize to you enough the importance of PRAYING IN THE SPIRIT, i.e. in tongues. When you do so, you are praying the *will* of the Father and He is able to do that which is impossible for us. Jesus said, *"The things which are impossible with men are possible with God."* (Luke 18:27).

Also, it is important to study the Word of God. If a person doesn't know the *word of God,* he has limited himself in knowing the *will of God.* Certainly God loves us and He loves to have us pray to Him, and He will answer every prayer He scripturally can, but sometimes our prayers might be out of our own hurt, negative feelings or even judgments. If we ask for things that are NOT God's will, God cannot and will not answer those prayers. Here is an unfortunate example of that.

A few months ago at a McDonald's, I struck up a conversation with a lady sitting near me, and she began to tell me rather angrily how someone had hurt her. After a time I suggested we pray about the situation. She agreed, but to my shock and alarm, she began to ask God to "hurt this person the way she hurt me," and "don't let her have any peace, but let her know what it feels like…etc."! I could not agree with that prayer, and additionally I knew God would not answer it because JESUS said "*Love* your enemies, *bless* those that curse you, *do good* to those that harm you, and *pray* for those that despitefully use you and persecute you." (Matthew 5:44). This is the Lord's way.

In other words, I knew *the will of God* in this case, because I knew *the word of God.* She had said she was a believer, so I gently told her what the Lord said and urged her to ask Him to bless the woman. This would help *her* be set free (from anger, bitterness, etc.) and would open the door for God to work in the situation; instead she quickly gathered her things, gave me a rather angry look, and left.BUT I have hope for her because Abba Daddy (God the Father) has "ways and means" of softening the hearts of His children to do His will. Paul wrote of himself and Apollos, "I planted, Apollos watered, but GOD gave the increase." (1 Corinthians 3:6). I believe God perhaps had me plant the thought (seed) of forgiveness, someone else will water it, and GOD will give the increase!

Study the word of God, read it, think about it. When you pray, in the spirit especially, scriptures and perhaps biblical incidents or even natural words will rise in your spirit (come to mind) that will lead you in how or what to pray for that situation. Then you will pray with authority, power, and faith based on the word of God—and you will get the answers to those prayers.

"Now this is the confidence we have in Him, that if we ask anything according to His will, He hears us. And if we know that He hears us, whatever we ask, we know that we have the petitions that we have asked of Him." **(I John 5:14–15), and** ***"The effectual fervent prayer of a righteous man avails (accomplishes, helps, forces along) much."*** **(James 5:16). Praise God!**

Chapter 6

I Didn't Even Go Near That Closet!

"Go to the sea, cast in a hook, and take the fish that comes up first. And when you have opened its mouth, you will find a piece of money; take that and give it to them for Me and you."
—Matthew 17:27

Last week the phone rang, and when I picked it up, my friend Taria's voice came over the line. "Donna, you know Jennifer who's moving in with me?" No, I didn't know Jennifer; but I knew *of* her. Taria had invited this young woman to stay with her for a few months to help her get back on her feet.

Taria continued, "Well, she's packing her things to move over and she's lost her keys. I've tried to pray with her about them two times, but each time it was like I couldn't pray and the Holy Spirit said, 'Call Donna.' I've called you two times today, but didn't get you. Jennifer and I were just talking about it and the Holy Spirit said again, 'Call Donna." Jennifer's right here; I'm going to put you on speaker phone."

Jennifer and I introduced ourselves over the phone then I said, 'I understand from Taria you've lost your keys. When was the last time you definitely knew you had them?"

"Last Saturday," she replied. "I used them when I went over to the house last Saturday to pack some things. I opened the front door with them." It was Wednesday evening now which meant they'd been missing five days. She explained she had been sick for two weeks prior to that, staying at her mother and step-dad's house. Her uncle had picked her up in his truck and driven her to her house to help her pack.

"When it was time to leave, I couldn't find them. My uncle and I searched the house. I even went through all the trash, thinking maybe I had accidently thrown them out. No keys."

Fortunately, thank God, she had a spare house key, so she was able to lock the house when they left. "I've been back over there two times looking for them, but I can't find them anywhere," she finished.

Well, since the Holy Spirit had told Taria to call me, I was pretty sure the keys would be found after we prayed. Why did He want *me* to pray? To even partially understand this, I think it's important to recognize that the Lord knows everything about us, including how we individually think.

Psalms 139:2–4 tells us *"You understand my thought afar off... and are acquainted with all my ways, for there is not a word in my mouth, but behold, O Lord, You know it altogether."* I believe this also means that He knows how we will react in any given situation if He chooses to know. He knew I would ask for something supernatural to get those keys back if necessary.

It was about 5:30 p. m. when I said, "Well, let's pray."

With empathy for her plight, I prayed that Jennifer would find her keys, also, "In the Name of Jesus, I *command* those keys to return to her or get themselves somewhere where she will find them!"

Then this thought came and I spoke it out, "Father, Abba Daddy, You can even *recreate* those keys if necessary. If they were thrown away or if someone else has found them, I ask You to have an angel get them and put them somewhere, like on the middle of a bed or wherever You choose, but someplace where she will know that only YOU could have done it, so You receive all the glory. We give You all the praise and glory for this, and we thank You for it, in JESUS' mighty name!"

I also asked that Jennifer would "put her hands on those keys, *today would be good, Lord,* at the latest by tomorrow so she can drop those keys into my hand tomorrow night! In Jesus' name, we thank You, Father!" Jennifer thanked me for praying and we hung up.

Well, I didn't hear from Jennifer or Taria all the next day. The enemy (Satan or one of his cohorts) tried to tell me the keys hadn't been found because "one of them would have called me if she had found them." Please note: the devil and his crew make their suggestions to us in "first person" statements so we will think the doubting (or angry or fearful, etc.) thoughts are our own, but they are not, and we do not have to receive them. I was unmoved by the negative thoughts; I was in *perfect peace* about those keys.

In fact, several times when negative thoughts came, I declared *out loud*, "'I walk by faith, not by sight,' Lord (2 Corinthians 5:7), and I *know* You have answered that prayer for those keys. I know in my spirit those keys will be found before church tonight!" Our church's midweek service was Thursday night; Jennifer had said she would come so we could meet.

Neither Taria nor Jennifer was at church that night, but I knew that whatever their reasons, the Lord was using this in me to test and stretch *my* faith. He likes to do that with us. In fact, the *longer* the delay, the *surer* I was about those keys. It may sound strange, but in the spirit I could actually "feel" the keys in my right hand. I could feel their weight and little sharp points against my palm.

After church that night, my cell phone rang. It was Taria. "Donna, she found them! Jennifer found her keys!"

"Praise the Lord! Where were they?" I asked.

"They were *underneath* her vacuum cleaner in the closet! She said she hasn't touched that vacuum cleaner for over a week!"

"Praise the Lord! God must have had an angel put them there! When did she find them?"

"*Last night* about 9:30, but she was so busy cleaning the house, she didn't call me. Then this morning I was praying with someone and had my phone turned off most of the day. She just called," Taria explained.

"She has more than just one or two keys on her key chain, right?" I asked.

"Oh, yeah! She's got a big bunch of keys, and some little keys too," Taria replied. We rejoiced together and thanked God for this amazing answer to prayer and for how quickly (four hours!) He had answered.

Jennifer later told me why she had been so desperate to find her keys. On the key chain were keys to the house she had been renting, the key to her mother and step-dad's house, keys to a beautiful home where she did house–sitting from time to time, keys to a business associate's office, and her *only* car key, a special kind that costs $125 to replace!

She also shared what had happened after we prayed that night.

She had gotten a ride back to the house to clean and search some more. Her little 5-lb dog was with her, and it barfed. She picked up the tiny mess with a paper towel, and "it looked fine, but then the thought came, 'Vacuum the floor; it will look better with the vacuum marks unbroken.'" (I believe the Holy Spirit spoke that to her.) So she went to the entry closet, opened the door, lifted the vacuum cleaner, and there were her keys—under the vacuum cleaner!

"Donna, I didn't even go near that closet the night my uncle was with me and hadn't touched the vacuum cleaner for over a week!"

Did God have an angel put them there? Did the keys move "of their own accord" as the iron gate did the night an angel led Peter out of prison? "When they were past the first and second guard posts, they came to the iron gate that leads to the city, which opened to them of its own accord; and they went out…" (Acts 12:10). We probably will never know how the keys got there until we are in heaven, but I believe GOD heard our prayer and answered in a way that only He could. To God be all the glory and thanks for this!

Now dear Reader, what's the big deal about finding her keys? By sharing this true story, I want to encourage *you* to start asking for miraculous answers to prayer, for things that only God can do. That way all the glory will go to Him. Also, if you feel led or inspired by the Holy

Spirit to *command* things to happen in Jesus' name, do that too. We have scriptural authority for this given by Jesus Himself. I'm going to share some examples of this in the next chapter.

"So Jesus said to them, '"assuredly, I say to you, if you have faith as a mustard seed, you will say to this mountain, 'Move from here to there,' and it will move, and nothing will be impossible for you."' **(Matthew 17:20). Thank You, Lord!**

Chapter 7

Jesus is Lord of the Molecules too!

The people that do know their God shall be strong and do exploits.
—Daniel 11:32

If you read my first book, *Run to the Battle: In Jesus' Name* (RTTB), you might remember the incident with my emergency cable. That incident changed my life. Years ago, while at a garage to get my car's new emergency cable installed, the mechanic told me, "It won't work! It's too little. You're gonna have to take it somewhere else or order a new one."

He pointed up to my car overhead where a long cable ran along under the axle, but stopped seven or eight inches from a short cable with a hook on it. He indicated they were supposed to hook together, but were too short.

Without any premeditation on my part, I simply said, "Let me pray," lifted my arm so that my hand was six to eight inches below the cables, and said firmly, "Metal, in JESUS' name, I *command* you to stretch, relax, and come together! In Jesus' name, you must lengthen and hook together!" Then I turned to the mechanic, gestured towards the cables and told him, "Try it now."

The mechanic reached up, grasped the cables with his pliers and pulled. As he did, both cables s-t-r-e-t-c-h-e-d, and he hooked them together. With a loud exclamation, his arms fell to his sides; he stumbled backwards and almost fell down. I was stunned too, in awe of what the Lord had done. It was the first time I had ever commanded an *inanimate object* to do something in Jesus' name, and it had *obeyed* me!

As he stared at me with his mouth open and fear on his face, these words just rose up in me and I declared to him, "Jesus is Lord of the molecules too!"

Well, that single incident was a turning point in my spiritual life. It opened a door of faith for me between the needs in this natural, visible world and the *inexhaustible resources* of the Kingdom of heaven that are available to the children of God from the heavenly, unseen realm that Jesus declared the sons of God could have access to—in His name. As I relived in memory seeing the cables actually s-t-r-e-t-c-h and lengthen, and the mechanic's reaction: amazement, fear, awe, something was happening in my spirit. In the following weeks and months, I was grasping or internalizing the truth that should have been obvious all along; Jesus *really meant it* when He said, *"If you have faith as a grain of mustard seed, you can say to this mulberry tree, 'Be pulled up by the roots and be planted in the sea,' and it would obey you!"* (Luke 17:6). The complete story is in my first book with some of the aftermath of that awesome experience.

I mention this incident because the Lord has given this authority to all His children and most of us have never taken one step down this road of speaking to *objects* in Jesus' name and commanding them to do certain things that are needful, legitimate, and would bring glory to GOD when we tell our friends and family about it. I have never spoken to an object for show; only when there is an actual, legitimate need. God's Holy Word warns us not to abuse holy things and *not* to test the LORD.

Remember when the devil tempted Jesus in the wilderness? One of the temptations was to show off His power. It is recorded "Then the devil took Him up into the holy city, set Him on the pinnacle (*highest point*) of the temple and said to Him, 'If you are the Son of God, throw Yourself down. For it is written "He shall give His angels charge concerning you" and 'in their hands they shall bear you up, lest you dash your foot against a stone' (Psalms 91:11–12).

Jesus responded, "It is written again, 'You shall not tempt the Lord your God.'" (Matthew 4:5–7).

I love how Jesus countered the devil when he quoted the word of God out of place and tried to get Jesus to do something that was contrary to God's will. Jesus shot right back "It is written again..." and quoted God's word with the correct application. Praise the Lord! That's another reason it's so important to study the word of God and know what it says. "Thy word I have hidden in my heart that I might not sin against You" (Psalms 119:11).

My point is *the Lord has given us the right or authority to speak to objects in HIS name,* and I believe, to circumstances as we are quickened by precious Holy Spirit. This would be for our or others' aid and for *God's* glory just as Peter, Phillip, Paul and many others did in the early church.

Peter, for example, spoke to the man who was lame from his mother's womb and said, *"Silver and gold I do not have, but what I do have I give you: In the name of Jesus Christ of Nazareth, rise up and walk.' And he took him by the right hand and lifted him up and his feet and ankle bones received strength. So he, leaping up, stood and walked and entered the temple with them—walking, leaping, and praising God."* (Acts 3:6-8)! Hallelujah!

What was it that Peter had? Well, we know he had FAITH—a deep faith in Jesus that He is the Son of God (Luke 9:20) and because of that, he had faith in everything Jesus said. So when Jesus said of those who believe in Him, *"They will lay hands on the sick and they will recover."* (Mark 16:17-18), Peter believed it and acted upon the Lord's word, and it happened just as Jesus had said it would. Praise to His holy Name!

I believe God will answer us with miracles also. These wonderful happenings will bring glory to God and stir up faith in others. Here is another example.

When we lived in southern California, one day my husband and I drove 60 miles to Escondido to visit my Dad. Ed's pickup had a definite problem; it sputtered and coughed and would almost stop for no obvious reason. He had been unable to locate and repair the problem.

On a long stretch of freeway passing through hills, the truck sputtered, slowed considerably, and we crawled along for several miles. When he saw an exit sign to a town 12 or 13 miles away, Ed exited to find a mechanic. The truck was barely running as we crawled along a winding country road. With plenty of time to think, I remembered how my emergency cable stretched and some other incidents after that, and finally said, "You know, Jesus said *'If we had faith as a mustard seed we can say to this mulberry tree, be pulled up by the roots and be planted in the sea, and it would obey you.'"* (Luke 17:6).

Then I suggested "Why don't we pray and tell the truck to run in Jesus' name?"

The response was what a lot of people might have, a quick look at me and an explanation as to why that wasn't going to work. "God has set up natural laws of physics and science that dictate the way things work. He is a God of order… I serve a God of order, and He operates within those laws." My request was thus dismissed.

Now, I know this sounds reasonable and logical, but God is so much greater than human reason and logic. He dwells outside this earth realm. He *created* the laws of physics and science and can suspend or change them at any time. As Jesus once said to His disciples, *"With men it is impossible, but not with God; for with God, all things are possible."* (Mark 10:27).

We continued in silence, except for the engine's stalling, revving, and sputtering. Well, I started thinking about what Jesus did while on earth. Several incidents came to mind: The time He wanted to feed about five thousand men besides women and children, so He multiplied five small loaves and two fishes, and they took up twelve baskets of leftovers (Matthew 14:20-21).

The time He sent the disciples ahead in a boat while He prayed alone, then came to them *walking on the water.* (Mark 6:48). Another time, He was asleep in a boat when a violent storm came up and the boat was sinking. The disciples were afraid and *"…awoke Him, and said, 'Master, do You not care that we are perishing?' Then He arose and rebuked the wind, and said to the sea, 'Peace, be still!' And the wind ceased and there was a great calm."* (Mark 4:36–39). I was quietly praying in tongues quite a lot as I thought on these things.

Suddenly, this all came together in one clear realization. *While on earth Jesus did not limit Himself to operating within the laws of physics and science!* When there was a need beyond the available, natural provision, He just moved or reached into the invisible, eternal realm and brought out whatever was needed to meet the need in this earthly realm! *"We do not look at the things that are seen, but at the things that are not seen. For the things which are seen are temporary, but the things which are not seen are eternal."* (2 Corinthians 4:18). I believe this is exercising the authority of the Kingdom of God, a privilege granted to His children.

Just then the truck sputtered again and almost stopped. Something rose up in me; I suddenly reached out and "laid hands" (both of them!) on the dash board. Words just came up inside me, and I spoke: "Truck, I command you in JESUS' name to stop this sputtering and crawling, and I tell you to Run Right, the way you're supposed to run. In Jesus' name, you shape up, Now!"

God is my witness—that truck made a noise like a big mechanical hiccup, "caught," picked up speed and ran along purring like a kitten. It never missed a beat after that. There was total silence in the cab, but not in my spirit. In my spirit I was rejoicing and praising God!

The change in the engine was so immediate, complete, and lasting that I wanted to share this with you, dear Reader. I believe that truck obeyed a command spoken by faith in JESUS and His Words—a command spoken in *His Name*. Here is another example.

When our son-in-law Mark was sent by the Army for his second tour to Germany, our daughter Laura and their three young sons followed about a month later. Mark's unit was deployed for six months to another area, so Laura had full care of the boys for six months. When they moved into their living quarters, she discovered the lock on the front door, the only outside door, was broken. When she requested its repair, the man she spoke to said, "The locksmiths are all on strike; we don't have anyone to send." With contractual workers, no one else was allowed to repair the lock.

So every time she left the house, she prayed that God would have an angel guard the door and keep everything safe. After two weeks of this, she got tired of praying for an angel every time she and the boys needed to go out, and it occurred to her, "Why don't I just pray and tell the lock to work?" (This was six or seven years after the incident with my emergency cable, which I had shared with all our children.) So my dear daughter, who is a woman of faith, went to the door, placed a hand on the lock, and *spoke* to it. "In the name of Jesus, line up and work properly—in Jesus' name!" Then she tried the lock and it worked!

It worked properly for more than three years while they were there, and she forgot about it until the last day, the day they were leaving. An inspection of quarters is always done when military folk leave and the inspector was there. After awhile she noticed he was standing by the front door fiddling with something. Finally he asked, "Have you been having any trouble with this lock?"

"No," she answered, but then remembered. "It wouldn't work when we first moved here, but I prayed over it in the name of Jesus, and told it to work, and it's worked for over three years." Well, it wasn't working now and he wrote up a repair order for it! Don't you love the way God does things? "Bless the Lord. O my soul, and all that is within me, and *forget not* all His benefits!" (Psalms 103:2).

If it hadn't stopped working that day, because the pray–er (Laura) was leaving, she might have forgotten about her prayer or, more rightly, her *command* to the lock to "line up and work properly—in Jesus' name!", and we wouldn't have this wonderful praise report to share with you, to give glory to God, and to encourage *you* to step out in faith. Begin to speak to the mountains and situations in your own life, dear Reader, and the lives of those you love. Remember too that Jesus said, "Love your neighbor *as yourself*." (Matthew 22:39).

I'll share one more example of God's willingness to honor His word and answer our prayers of faith with "impossible" things. (There are additional incidents that people have shared with me after they read RTTB and spoke to some things themselves, in Jesus' Name! So far, the events have all had to do with recovering lost things and equipment suddenly working.) By the way, plants and animals are very responsive to blessings and commands given to them in the name of Jesus. Praise the Lord!

Joan Luckey, my dear friend in central California, gave a copy of *RTTB* to a Teen Challenge center for women where she teaches a class. The next time she came, the women were all rejoicing and praising God. The director told her what had happened.

That day the director had read about my emergency cable stretching and also about one of my friends who had been cooking on one burner and a hot plate for six months, because three burners and the oven didn't work on her old stove! In October that year, she had heard me tell about my emergency cable stretching and *kept thinking* about it. I'm sure the Holy Spirit was preparing her for a miracle because the night before Thanksgiving, she went to her kitchen, laid hands on her old stove and, in JESUS' name, *commanded it* to "work and cook her

Thanksgiving dinner the next day." The next morning everything worked! The oven and all four burners worked all day, and she cooked a delicious meal. The day after only the one burner worked again.

Well, the director told Joan the dryer at the center hadn't been working, and they didn't have funds for a new one. After reading several of these accounts, she asked one of the residents to pray with her for the broken down dryer. They laid hands on it, commanded it to work "in JESUS' name," pushed the button, and it started! All the residents were laughing and praising God when Joanie got there.

If Jesus is your Lord and Savior, dear Reader, you have the same right and authority to do what these have done. So, by faith start speaking to things. Also, based on God's word, in Jesus' name, you can ask God to send angels to help you and others. Hebrews 1:14 says of angels, "Are they not all ministering spirits sent forth to minister to those who will inherit salvation?" God sends them when we ask. He loves you—ask Him!

"And seeing a fig tree by the road, He came to it and found nothing on it but leaves, and said to it, 'Let no fruit grow on you ever again.' And immediately the fig tree withered away. Now when the disciples saw it, they marveled … So Jesus answered and said to them, 'Assuredly, I say to you, if you have faith and do not doubt, you will not only do what was done to the fig tree, but also if you say to this mountain, "Be removed and be cast into the sea," it will be done. And all things, whatever you ask in prayer, believing, you will receive.'" **(Matthew 21:19–22). Thank You, Lord Jesus! You are Wonderful!**

Chapter 8

The Doctors Have Said We Can't Have a Baby

A good man's steps are ordered by the Lord
and He delights in his way.
—Psalms 37:23

Quite often through the vehicle of ordinary circumstances, God does extraordinary things—and at times He will let *you* be a part of it! Personally, based on the above scripture, I think He enjoys doing this. If you know God, by this I mean, if you are a person of faith and the Word, sometimes when you are just minding your own business, God is setting you up to mind *His* business. When this happens, an ordinary day changes to extraordinary—one you will remember the rest of your life.

A good example of this is recorded in I Samuel 9.

"There was a man of Benjamin whose name was Kish... and he had a son whose name was Saul... Now the donkeys of Kish, Saul's father, were lost. And Kish said to his son Saul, 'Please take one of the servants with you, and arise, go and look for the donkeys.'

"So he passed through the mountains of Ephraim and through the land of Shalisha, but they did not find them. Then they passed through the land of Shaalim, but they were not there. Then he passed through the land of the Benjamites, but they did not find them.

"When they had come to the land of Zuph, Saul said to his servant who was with him, 'Come, let us return, lest my father cease caring about the donkeys and become worried about us.'

"And he said to him, 'Look now, there is in this city a man of God… all that he says surely comes to pass. So let us go there; perhaps he can show us the way we should go." He was speaking of Samuel the prophet of God.

"…So they went up to the city. And as they were coming into the city, there was Samuel, coming out toward them on his way up to the high place.

"Now the Lord had told Samuel in his ear the day before Saul came, saying, 'Tomorrow about this time I will send you a man from the land of Benjamin, and you shall anoint him commander over My people Israel, that he may save My people from the hand of the Philistines, for I have looked upon My people, because their cry has come to Me.'

"And when Samuel saw Saul, the Lord said to him, 'There he is, the man of whom I spoke to you. This one shall reign over My people.'"

Wouldn't it be wonderful to have God say of you; "There he is," or "There she is"? "This is the one that shall visit My people in prison, feed My little children, take the gospel to a land far away, or... ?" What an honor for God to send *you* in answer to the cry (prayer) of someone else! I believe He is still doing this today. Of course, He Himself will guide you in what to do, *"for it is God who works in you both to will and to do for His good pleasure."* (Philippians 2:13).

Later, you realize the LORD had it planned from the beginning, and you were just privileged to have a part in His plan. He placed you exactly where He wanted you, when He wanted you there for His good pleasure and purpose.

To understand this, one must accept that the Lord knows us inside out. He knows our gifts, talents, training, interests, and how we will react in any given situation. Psalms 139 is one of my favorite scripture portions. Verses 1–5 are so beautiful:

"O Lord, You have searched me and known me. You know my sitting down and my rising up. You understand my thought afar off. You comprehend my path and my lying down, and are acquainted with all my ways. For there is not a word on my tongue, But behold, O Lord, You know it altogether."

So you see how easy it is for the Lord to put us in a situation where He wants to do certain things because He knows just how we will react and what we will do about it! If you are close to Him, know His word, and are led by the Holy Spirit, He will guide you in God's will for the occasion.

As I pray in the spirit about specific needs, quite often I "see" myself or others doing certain things, or pertinent scriptures will come to mind, i.e. rise in my spirit, so that is what I tell the person to do, or do myself, or pray. This is being led by the Holy Spirit. *"Thy word is a lamp unto my feet; a light unto my path."* (Psalms 119:105). Let me give you a personal example; I believe the year was 1980.

"We want to have a baby," the young couple looked earnestly at my husband and me across the tiny table in their kitchen. Ed and I were the only two who had shown up for the twice–monthly Bible study and fellowship meeting in their home that Friday evening. This had never happened before, and never happened again—that we were the only two who came. They invited us to the kitchen where we sat at their table with filled coffee mugs and a plate of cookies in front of us. After a few minutes, the talk turned to things of the Lord. They then confided a deep heartache they had never shared in the group meeting. I'll call them Michael and Michelle.

"We've been married twelve years," Michael said. "The first two years we used birth control, but then we wanted to start a family, so we stopped using it, but nothing happened. After a year, we went to a doctor, and after tests, were told we couldn't have a baby. We went to another doctor for a second opinion; but the results were the same. The doctors have said we can't have a baby."

He paused. "We know doctors don't have the last word; God does. But we don't know if it's God's *will* for us to have a baby or not."

Michelle added, "We have nieces and nephews that we love so much, and we buy things for them that their parents can't afford, so we're wondering if it's God's will for us to just help them and not have any children of our own." Her sweet face looked so forlorn.

As they were speaking, scriptures started rising up in my spirit such as "God said to them, 'Be fruitful and multiply...'" (Genesis 1:28); "... children are a heritage of the Lord and the fruit of the womb is His reward." (Psalms 127:3), and others.

Finally, they looked at me and asked, "Would you pray for us to have a baby?" and hesitantly added, "We really would like to have a little girl."

By this time the word of God regarding children was sounding loudly and clearly in my spirit, and I felt it was God's Will for them to have a baby. When the Holy Spirit brings scripture or biblical incidents to you while you're praying, He is revealing to you God's Will for that person or situation. *The Holy Spirit uses the word of God to reveal the will of God.* Sometimes a natural word might also be given or a picture, even a fragrance. This could give additional understanding and direct you on how or what to pray.

It is wonderful praying the written word of God on a specific subject. If the word resonates in your spirit, is *alive* in your spirit, then when you open your mouth the words will flow forth "clothed" with faith. You will speak with an authority and assurance that what is being spoken WILL BE. This anointing of the Holy Spirit enables one to know, say, and do things beyond one's own strength, wisdom, or ability. This is what happened that evening.

By the time I finished praying, faith had filled our hearts and the atmosphere was supercharged with expectation and joy. The presence of God was over and around us. With a laughing joy, I told them, "Jesus was the only One conceived by the Holy Spirit, so now you two have to do your part!" and we all laughed. They told us they'd keep us posted. Ed and I left rejoicing, expecting a good report.

Well, three weeks later *to the day*, on Friday afternoon, I received a phone call from Michelle. Excitedly, she said, "Donna, we think I'm pregnant! We just did a little home test that can tell if you're only a few days along, and it's positive, but I've got an appointment with the doctor on Monday. We'll let you know."

You can probably guess the results. Nine and a half months after that prayer meeting, they had a bouncing baby boy. Praise the Lord! Later events proved, however, that God wasn't through blessing their family yet. Why did it take 13 years before they had their first child? I don't know, but I do know God is sovereign. He is good, and His timing is perfect. He does all things well. One thing about it, the way God did it they knew their wonderful son was from God, an answer to prayer!

"But as for me, I trust in You, O Lord; I say, 'You are my God.' My times are in your hand" and "Be of good courage, and He shall strengthen your heart, all you who hope in the Lord." **(Psalms 31:14-15a, 24). Hallelujah!**

Chapter 9

Oh God, Give Them a Baby Girl!

In all the land were found no women so beautiful as the daughters of Job; and their father gave them an inheritance among their brothers.
—Job 42:15

God is very gracious and He not only has a plan for each of us, He also knows what is *best* for us. Sometimes God answers prayer in ways we don't expect.

I once read of a minister who wanted to do something for the children of a Chinese orphanage. He asked them what they wanted and they all said "A swimming pool!" That was not what he expected because they had need of so many basic necessities, but when he prayed about it, the Lord told him to build them the pool, so he did. A few years later the orphanage and surrounding area were in a raging flood, but because of the pool, all the children and staff knew how to swim and not one life of those at the orphanage was lost! Praise the Lord!

Well, back to Michael and Michelle, time had passed and they were going to a different church. I hadn't seen them for several years when I received an invitation to a 'sales" party at their home for the coming Monday night.

Since I had a Monday night commitment (prayer with Doc Holleman and Irlene Shearer) which I shared about in my first book), I called and agreed to drop by on Wednesday and look at the catalog. Michelle told me on the phone that day, "Donna, Ryan (*not their son's real name*) is five years old now. We've been trying to have another baby for over three years. Please remember us in your prayers."

The next day, I was thinking about Michelle's request and started praying in tongues about it. Suddenly a strong desire rose up in me, "Oh God, give them another baby and let it be a baby GIRL—and let her be as one of the daughters of Job who were the fairest in the land! Thank You, Father, in Jesus' name!" Job 42:15 tells us *"...in all the land, were no women found so fair as the daughters of Job."* (KJV).

When I arrived at their home Wednesday afternoon, I told Michelle about the prayer God had given me for a baby girl for them. Her response was unexpected. "We had wanted a girl the first time, but we love Ryan so much that now we want another boy."

Though surprised, I thought "*Well, it doesn't matter to me whether they have a boy or girl, so I'll just pray and ask the Lord for a boy for them.*" But that wasn't God's Plan!

What we pray or ask God for is important. The Word tells us *"Now this is the confidence we have in Him, that if we ask anything according to His will, He hears us. And if we know that if He hears us, whatever we ask, we know that we have the petitions we have asked of Him."* (I John 5:14–15). Hallelujah! But at that point in my Christian walk, I didn't realize that the Lord had already revealed His will in this matter, so I naively said, "Ok, let's pray."

God is very merciful for I had just decided to pray *against* His will, but, praise God, He held me back from it. It is recorded in the Bible that God did this for someone else—a king. King Abimelech had been told by Abraham, who was "God's friend," that his wife Sarah was his sister (she was his half–sister). Sarah was very beautiful and Abraham was afraid the king would kill him for Sarah if he knew she was his wife. The incident is recorded in Genesis 20:2–18.

"Now Abraham said of Sarah his wife, 'She is my sister.' And Abimelech king of Gerar sent and took Sarah.

"But God came to Abimelech in a dream by night, and said to him, 'Indeed you are a dead man because of the woman whom you have taken, for she is a man's wife.'

"But Abimelech had not come near her; and he said, 'Lord, will You slay a righteous nation also? Did he not say to me, "She is my sister"? And she, even she herself said, 'He is my brother.' In the integrity of my heart and innocence of my hands, I have done this.'

"And God said to him in a dream, 'Yes, I know that you did this in the integrity of your heart. For I also withheld you from sinning against Me; therefore I did not let you touch her. Now, therefore, restore the man's wife; for he is a prophet, and he will pray for you and you shall live. But if you do not restore her, know that you shall surely die, you and all who are yours.'

"So Abimelech rose early in the morning, called all his servants, and told all these things in their hearing; and the men were very afraid." I would be very afraid too! Hebrews 10:31 tells us, *"It is a fearful thing to fall into the hands of the living God."*

Just to finish the story, *"Then Abimelech took sheep, oxen, and male and female servants, and gave them to Abraham; and he restored Sarah his wife to him... Then to Sarah he said, 'Behold, I have given your brother a thousand pieces of silver; indeed this vindicates you before all who are with you and before all others.' Thus she was reproved." After all, at her husband's request she had lied to his face!*

"So Abraham prayed to God and God healed Abimelech, his wife, and his maidservants. Then they bore children; for the Lord had closed up the wombs of the house of Abimelech because of Sarah, Abraham's wife." Children are a blessing, a gift from God! See Psalms 127:3–5.

Well, God knew it was "in the integrity of my heart" that I was going to pray the opposite of His revealed will, but praise God, He withheld me from it also. I knelt there by the coffee table in their living room and began to pray aloud, intending to ask for another boy for them, but though I tried every way I could to ask for a boy, I *could not do it.* The Holy Spirit simply would NOT let me ask for a boy.

I prayed about "this precious little one" that God had for them. I thanked Him for the "little darling" and "the little sweetheart" He was going to give them. I asked Him to bless this "new little life" that was coming into their family, **etc.**, and all the while the desire (more like a mandate!) to ask for a little *girl* was growing inside me.

If you can imagine a balloon inside you that is being blown up, getting bigger and bigger by the moment, that is what was happening with me. The more I prayed, the stronger the desire to ask for a little girl grew. It was like trying to hold a lid on a pressure cooker to NOT pray that prayer until finally I could stand it no longer.

I jumped to my feet, lifted both hands toward heaven, and shouted, "Oh God, give them a baby! And let it be a baby GIRL—and let her be as one of the daughters of Job who were the fairest in the land! Thank You, Father, in JESUS' mighty name!"

Whew, what a relief! It was like the balloon had popped. Suddenly it was spoken or prayed out loud and I felt a tremendous release in my spirit and knew it was *done.* They were going to have a baby; she was going to be a little girl, and she was going to be beautiful.

Oh, one other thing Michelle told me that day, "Donna, we have many people praying for us to have another baby. For a long time we've asked our family, friends, and friends at church to pray and they all said they would. They keep telling us 'We're praying for you,' but you're the only one who prayed *with* us right then."

I think there's something to learn here. If someone asks you to pray for them about something or to "remember them in prayer," pray for them then and there. You might forget to do it later. Even if you're in a public place, you can say "Let's do it right now; you don't need to close your eyes. We'll just look as though we're talking, but we'll be praying to God." I have prayed with people this way many times—probably many of you have too.

Anyway, about a month after Michelle and I had prayed, our oldest daughter, Deborah, came home from her job at Barro's Pizza and said, "Mom, 'Michelle Rogers' came in for a pizza tonight and said, 'Tell your mother I'm not pregnant yet.'"

This surprised me because the anointing from the Lord had been so clear and strong that I had expected her to become pregnant within a few days like the first time. The next day as I was driving to Diamond Bar, a nearby community, I was praying in tongues about this and sort of questioned the Lord about it. "Lord, she's not pregnant yet?"

And just like that, in my spirit I heard, "If she were pregnant now, the baby would be born in November and they don't want the baby born in November."

"Oh," from me. This was totally unexpected, a revelation in fact. I immediately started counting the months on my fingers as I drove along. It was true; eight months more brought us to November.

That evening I called Michelle and told her about my prayer and what the Holy Spirit had said. Instantly she replied, "That's right! We have seven or eight birthdays in our families in November and December. We don't want the baby born in November or December."

Gently I asked her, "Well, when would you like for the baby to be born?" (God has so much patience with us, dear Reader.)

There was a pause while she thought about it then she said, "After the holidays."

We prayed together and I asked the Lord to "Please let the baby be born after the holidays. Thank You, in Jesus' name."

God is so gracious. A few months passed and Michelle called to tell me the good news that she was pregnant. I was excited. "Praise the Lord! What's the due date?"

"January 2nd." The day *after* the holidays!

The exactness of God's timing amazes me. Believe it or not, their beautiful little daughter was born on her due date, January 2nd. I was invited to the baby shower, which was before her birth, and along with the gift gave them a little card on which I had written the scripture in Job.

I don't know why God let me be a part of their two miracles. It was God's doing, not mine. Maybe it was because He knew I would write it in a book one day and it would encourage others to not give up because they have been told they can't have children.

God is a miracle-working God. He loves you. Seek to discern His will for your circumstance. Ask Him for a miracle in Jesus' name. If you don't have faith for one, ask Him to send someone to pray with you who does have faith for your miracle.

***"Every good gift and every perfect gift is from above, and comes down from the Father of lights, with whom there is no variation or shadow of turning, Of His own will He brought us forth by the word of truth…"* (James 1:17-18a). Thank You, Abba Daddy!**

Chapter 10

I Felt It Go Out Through My Feet

Therefore do not cast away your confidence,
which has great reward, For you have need of endurance,
so that after you have done The will of God,
you may receive the promise.
— Hebrews 10:35–36

So much of our walk with the Lord is by FAITH. We must learn to move in faith that He is leading us and speak out and declare things by faith. *"For we walk by faith and not by sight."* (2 Corinthians 5:7).

Let me give you an example of declaring something by faith, its being received by faith, but being lost by relying on "senses." It was sad.

In our home Bible fellowship group, there was a brother who frequently asked for prayer for his back because he had rheumatoid arthritis and was in a lot of pain. He often asked for prayer regarding his work situation also because he worked with three other men who were not believers and they seemed to "gang up" on him. In his words, they were sarcastic to him and made jokes about him to each other because he read his Bible at lunchtime.

Another problem was, because of his back, he couldn't lift boxes and carry them like the others (he had a doctor's excuse), so he couldn't really pull his weight on that part of the job, though it was not the primary duty of their work.

One Friday night after the Bible study had ended and we were having refreshments, several of us were talking and he mentioned again that his back was hurting—he was in severe pain. I asked if I could anoint him with oil and pray for him to be healed, he said, "Yes." I got the little bottle of anointing oil out of my purse, and with several others standing in a circle around him, I anointed his forehead with oil and began to pray in English and in tongues. The others prayed also, simultaneously but quietly.

All of a sudden, in the spirit I "saw" his skeleton, full sized, as he stood in front of me. I saw the arthritis in his joints as black "filings," like powder or super-fine black "grains" accumulated in his joints. It was in all his major joints to some degree: neck, shoulders, elbows, knees, but lay especially thick along his mid-to-lower spine. Precious Holy Spirit showed it. This was a "word of knowledge" as the Bible talks about in 1 Corinthians 12:7–8.

In prayer, I described to the others what the Holy Spirit was revealing, then *strongly* with authority and righteous indignation which I know was from the Holy Spirit, said "Arthritis, in Jesus' name, I command you to leave his body! GO OUT THROUGH HIS FEET, go to the pit and stay there—in JESUS' name!"

In the spirit, I "saw" those black filings rush along his bones. The ones in his arms rushed up to his shoulders, crossed to his neck, and with the black filings there, sped down his spine. The thicker accumulations along his spine were sucked out when the filings passed and the black mass rushed out through his feet. This all happened in a second or two.

He exclaimed, "It's gone! I felt it go. It went out through my feet—I felt it go out through my feet! It's gone!" He said this with wonder and joy. We were all praising the Lord.

Well, for three or four meetings (we met twice a month), every time he and his wife came, he told us happily that he was still well; he didn't have any pain, his arthritis was gone. We all praised God with him.

Then one Friday night when they came in, he was walking stiffly, sat down with difficulty, and before the meeting began, looked at me and announced, "It's back." While his wife looked at me rather reproachfully, he said that on Wednesday night after they were in bed, his back began to hurt "as bad as it had ever been at its worse. I turned to my wife and said, 'It's back.'" It had been hurting him ever since.

While he was talking, I was listening to him with one ear and for the Holy Spirit's insight with the other. When he finished, something occurred to me and I asked, "Did you ever tell those three men you work with, the ones who are so hard on you, that the Lord healed your back?"

"Well, no," he replied. "I was waiting to see if I stayed healed—to see if it would last before I said anything to them about it."

In that moment the Holy Spirit spoke to my spirit, "Do not pray for his healing anymore."

The Holy Spirit showed me it was easy to come to our group and praise God for his healing because we were all believers and we believed God had healed him. It was something else to tell unbelievers that Jesus had healed him by His Word and by His Spirit. That would have been a real declaration of faith. I am guessing he also did not start lifting and carrying boxes in those weeks either because he wouldn't have wanted to lose his doctor's excuse if he were "waiting to see if it would last."

The Lord wanted to use his testimony to draw those men to Himself. He wanted to display His goodness and power to them. It would have demonstrated to them His ability and *willingness* to heal where doctors could not, but He didn't get to because His child had timidly waited "to see if it lasted."

"Now the just shall live by faith, but if anyone draws back, My soul has no pleasure in him." (Hebrews 10:38). That is GOD speaking! Do you see it says, "NOW the just shall live by faith…"? When we SEE Him after earthly death or the "catching away," we won't need faith because then it will have become sight. We live by faith NOW.

I know the enemy "comes not but to steal, kill, and destroy," and in every instance when God answers prayer with a miracle, the devil comes to sow doubt, unbelief, intellectual arguments, and "logical" explanations, in order to steal the blessing.

I believe the Lord showed me what happened with that brother. As I mourned for him (somewhat as Samuel mourned for Saul after Saul was rejected as king by God), I "saw" this vision; he and his wife were lying in bed at night. A black "demon spirit of arthritis" came into the room and stretched over him. It put all the aches and pains of rheumatoid arthritis on him "as bad as he had ever had it" and waited to see what he would do.

What he should have done was declare by FAITH something like this: "By Jesus' stripes, I am healed! Satan, get your lying symptoms off me right now—in Jesus' name! I REFUSE this pain, and I refuse you, you lying spirit of rheumatoid arthritis. The LORD has healed me! Get out of here and never come back—in JESUS' name!" If he had done that, it would have lifted off him and left! You have to stand firm on these truths.

Instead, in the vision and in reality according to his own words, he turned to his wife and declared, "It's back!" That was what the demon wanted, and all it needed. He had just ACCEPTED it, thereby giving it permission to stay and torment him. I saw it just "settle in" on him while hurting him as badly as it could. (Believers can be "harassed," but not possessed.)

Now you might wonder; how could God do that? Why did the Holy Spirit tell you not to pray for his healing again? Well, God "lets" a lot of things happen that are not His "perfect will" for someone. For example: God *"is not willing that any should perish, but that all should come to repentance."* (2 Peter 3:9b), but many do perish because *their will* is to not repent. That's a choice. God has given us free will; we can choose to do things that hurt ourselves or others, or on the other hand, we can make choices that bring great blessings to ourselves, our families, and others.

Actions have consequences; decisions set courses. The consequences of stupid, ignorant, or even deceived choices will stand. Remember Adam and Eve? He sinned willfully; she was deceived. *"And Adam was not deceived, but the woman being deceived, fell into transgression."* (1 Timothy 2:14). Believe me, dear Reader, their decision to disobey God and eat from the Tree of the Knowledge of Good and Evil has affected every person of every generation. Actually, it affected all of creation. It is so important to be guided in our decisions by the word of God, led by the Holy Spirit.

When that brother refused to give glory to God for his healing, but decided instead to "wait and see if it lasted," he moved right out of faith into the realm of feeling and seeing. He drew back in his faith and it brought no glory to God.

Do you live by faith in the Son of God through grace and by the Spirit do mighty things for God? You will keep your miracle of healing the same way you received it—by faith.

"But without faith it is impossible to please Him, for he who comes to God must believe that He is, and that He is a rewarder of those who diligently seek Him." **(Hebrews 11:6). Praise the Lord!**

CHAPTER 11

HEALING IS THE CHILDREN'S BREAD

And when they had prayed, the place
where they were assembled together was shaken,
and they were all filled with the Holy Spirit,
And they spoke the word of God with boldness.
— Acts 4:31

I am going to jump ahead now and share something that happened at a later time as part of a sequence of amazing events, but because God taught me some things about healing through this experience, I want to include it here before I move on to another topic.

I have been in three automobile accidents and God brought a blessing out of each one, eventually. The first one was a head-on collision when Satan tried to kill me. Besides that I have been in two cars that were rear-ended. In the first one, I was sitting in the backseat behind the driver when we were hit from behind. I actually believe God allowed that in order to answer a prayer of mine that I will tell about later, but right now, I want to share what He taught me about *healing* through that experience.

The accident happened in October, 1991, in southern California where we lived then, and I was released from doctor's care in the spring of 1992. Even though I was released from the doctor's care and received a settlement, I was not healed. My back, neck, right arm, and shoulder hurt every day with a burning sensation deep in the muscles. This continued all summer and into the fall.

In October, our daughter Deborah's mother-in-law, Jane, called me. "Donna, Benny Hinn is coming to the Long Beach Convention Center in November. None of my friends will go with me to hear him. Will you go with me?" (Many of her friends were of Baptist persuasion and not familiar with divine healing back then.)

My immediate, glad response was, "Yes!"

So on the appointed day, I drove to her home and rode with her to Long Beach. The Convention Center was filled with people. After a long period of high praise and worship, Benny reverently said, "He's here. The Holy Spirit is here. Ask Him for whatever you need."

That morning when I had awaken, I was already hurting, and I had said, "Lord, I'm so tired of my back, neck, arm, and shoulder hurting." In fact, it had gotten to the point where I couldn't lift my right arm above my head without pain, but held it low without extending it very much. So when Benny said, "Ask Him for whatever you need," I silently prayed, "Lord, please heal my back, neck, arm, and shoulder. Thank You!" and continued to worship Him with thousands of others while glorious worship music was all around us. About 20 minutes later, I realized I had both arms fully extended above my head, worshipping Him. I was healed! Praise the Lord! So, five months after getting an answer-to-prayer-based-on-scripture settlement, God healed me! (I will tell you about that prayer later; I believe it is important.)

In December, my dear friend, Joan Luckey (Chapter Seven), invited Ed, Torrey, Christina and me to a beautiful Christmas program at Melodyland Christian Center in Anaheim where she worked. After the program, before we left for a Christmas party at Jim's and her home, I went into Melodyland's bookstore. As I looked around, knowing I had only a few minutes before we needed to leave, I silently prayed, "Lord, if there's any book here for me, please lead me to it. I don't have time to go through hundreds of books. Thank You!"

Then I started slowly walking down an aisle of books looking at the titles as I walked. Nothing drew my attention. I got to the end, turned, and started up the next aisle, books on both sides. I was praying in tongues, looking up and down, slowly searching the shelves when my eyes fell on a name I recognized, Dr. Richard Eby.

I had seen Dr. Eby on Trinity Broadcasting Network (TBN) a number of times and had his first book, *Caught up Into Paradise*, which tells the story of when he died and went to heaven. He had fallen from a balcony onto his head, which had cracked open. For his family's sake, doctors had pushed grey matter back in and closed his skull with 196 stitches, so he would "look better for the funeral!"

A lovely black lady working next door heard the fall, saw him lying on the ground, and called for an ambulance; she then called her pastor and asked him to alert their prayer chain. Dr. Eby's wife called their pastor, Dr. Ralph Wilkerson, and they also started praying he would live. Soon six prayer chains were praying for him. Meanwhile, Dr. Eby was in heaven with Jesus, when suddenly he was sent back to earth into his body. The Lord sent him back and later told him, "With your hands you will heal." Most of this is in his first book *Caught Up Into Paradise*, but that night I saw another book by him, *Didn't You Read My Book?,* which I promptly bought.

This book was a gift from God that I believe He led me to because He wanted to teach me how to *keep* my healing. In this book, Dr. Eby said that after his return, he would share his story, lay hands on people, pray for them, and they would be healed. But sometimes he would go back the next year, and some he had prayed for would have "lost" their healing—the disease or condition would be back. This kept happening over the course of several years, and it greatly concerned him. Why did people lose their healings?

So he set himself to fast and pray about this. I won't go into the amazing details, but in short, Jesus told him, "Give us this day our daily bread" was the key. Healing is part of the children's *bread* and we receive our healing the same way we receive our daily bread-—*daily*. We keep it by praising God and thanking Him for it daily.

Dr. Eby was stunned. Basically his response (not his words) was-- Lord, I've never heard this before! I can't go around telling people this. I need confirmation! The word of God says, *"In the mouth of two or three witnesses every word will be confirmed."* (2 Corinthians 13:1).

Dear Reader, you have a right, perhaps even a duty in some cases, to ask the Lord to *confirm* what He's told you. He will confirm it; He has for me so many times.

Dr. Eby proposed to test this by Not praising and thanking God for his healing. He had been brought back to life, healed, and commissioned to preach the gospel, and heal people. He was giving his testimony frequently, praising and thanking God continually, both publically and privately, witnessing to what the Lord had done.

In essence he said to Jesus—I have to see if this is really from You. I've got to test this, so I'm going to stop thanking and praising You for healing me. I want to see what happens. So starting this morning, I'm not going to thank and praise You any more for healing me. (He still had his medical practice at this time.)

Well, on Day 1, he made his rounds at the hospital and clinic as usual. On Day 2, he woke up aching, vision blurred, legs stiff, arms tingling. etc. He had a rough day at the office. Day 3, he couldn't walk, had to crawl to the bathroom, and back to bed. Discs in his back had compressed and fiery pains were shooting through his body. His vision was jumping around, and more. He couldn't go to the office at all. Day 4, he was barely alive, lying in bed unable to move his arms or legs with a loud ringing in his ears. He couldn't speak, his heartbeat was erratic.

Background information: After he had come back to life, before he was released from the hospital, the doctors had told his wife about his numerous internal and external injuries, including a broken back. As for his brain, well, it was unbelievable it could function at all, except that he *was* alive! Remember, his head had cracked open and doctors had brushed leaves and twigs off exposed *grey matter,* pushed it back into his head, and stitched his skull together! Basically they had told his wife, "We can't explain why he isn't dead. He could die any time."

Now, these years later, lying there unable to move, through jumbled vision, Dr. Eby saw his wife sitting by his bed, crying, and realized, "My wife thinks I'm dying! She doesn't know this is an experiment." Silently he shouted, "Jesus! The experiment worked but I hurt my dear wife. Please replace the miracle You did for me months ago. I praise and thank you for that marvelous recovery! …

restore me quickly so I can go to work and tell others about the *holding* power of praise and thanksgiving! Hallelujah! Thank You for being my Savior day by day!"

He wrote "An hour later I was at work in my office, as fit as before. ...Yes, Jesus had meant what He said!"

Dear Reader, I pray that you grasp this and will praise and thank the Lord when He has healed you. It has helped me so many times and I have shared this with many people through the years. I believe it is one of the keys of the Kingdom, a primary, but little-known principle of the Kingdom of God as it relates to healing. "Give us this day our daily bread!"

"Bless the Lord, O my soul, and all that is within me, bless His holy name! Bless the Lord, O my soul, and forget not all His benefits: Who forgives all your iniquities, Who heals all your diseases, Who redeems your life from destruction, Who crowns you with loving-kindness and tender mercies, Who satisfies your mouth with good things, so that your youth is renewed like the eagle's." **(Psalms 103:1-5)! Thank You, Jesus and Hallelujah!**

Chapter 12

I Don't Have to Thank God Every Day

So Jesus answered and said, "Were there not ten cleansed? But where are the nine? Were there not any found who returned to give glory to God except this foreigner?"
—Luke 17:17–18

During the time that some of these events happened, our pastor was led to initiate 24-hours-a-day prayer seven days a week, for an indefinite period. He asked everyone to sign up for a three-hour prayer watch during the week and continue until the Lord told him it was completed. People could pray at the church building or in their homes. Doc, Irlene, and I were still praying up in the Prayer Room on Monday nights; the sanctuary was used for the prayer watches.

I chose Friday nights between midnight and 3 a.m. because it was an open time slot and Ed could be home with Christina, 5, and Torrey, 9, at the time. There was a woman in the church, well loved and respected, who has since gone home to the Lord, who inquired about my time on the schedule and asked me to come to her home so we could pray together. I will call her Desiree. We had some remarkable times of prayer together.

She had been a singer and night club entertainer before coming to the Lord. She had a beautiful, powerful voice and frequently sang solos at church, songs which she had written herself—songs with a certain "swing" to them. While a professional singer, she had fallen and badly injured her foot. This or perhaps the fall itself had caused severe back problems for her.

A few months before we started praying together, she had had another back surgery, her sixth I believe, and was missing church because of it. One night when I arrived, she told me her back was really hurting. She said, "My last surgery was six months ago, and it still hasn't healed. The doctor told me it should have only taken two months, but it's infected, and he can't understand why the infection isn't healing. Will you pray for my back?"

I laid my hand on her lower back where it was hurting, and as I began to pray, it jumped or moved under my hand. The Holy Spirit revealed a small demon crouched in the area where she had had the surgery. I must have put my hand right on top of it when I started to pray! The Holy Spirit revealed it was there to keep the site infected and the incision from healing. I commanded it to go, but it resisted. Desiree said, "It doesn't want to go. It says the big demons assigned it there, and if it leaves, they'll kill it."

I said, "I thought demons couldn't die."

"It says you don't understand," she replied.

Please note: often times when a person is being delivered, he/she hears what the demon says. This is quite common in deliverance. Sometimes a demon might speak *through* the person—this is when possession is strong, but usually the demon speaks *to* the person to relay anything it might want to say, if you allow it to speak. Facial distortion, jerking, etc. is also common. In my experience not every demon can speak, but will show its activity or assignment if commanded to in Jesus' name. For example, if a person's ears begin to twitch, there is probably a spirit of deafness there, or if their hands turn bright red, this could indicate the person has been doing something *unclean* with his/her hands. In that case the person should confess it, and ask God for forgiveness, then you or sometimes the person him/herself can easily cast out the demon. It seems when they are revealed or their assignment known, it weakens their ability to resist. (And they *will* try to resist leaving.)

Please ask the Holy Spirit to reveal to you what is manifesting (revealing itself) and to lead you in what needs to be done. Coughing, sneezing, sighing are indicators that demons are leaving, as is vomiting. Don't be afraid of things like this, dear Reader. Jesus is So Much Greater than these created beings. He is the *Creator* and He is in us! "All things were made through Him, and without Him nothing was made that was made" (John 1:3). He has given us authority to Cast Them Out in His name!

The first time I did deliverance, it was thrust upon me. I had been asked to anoint a room and Irlene went with me—and the person started manifesting right there in front of us! It was pretty exciting, actually. The Lord led me that first time to bind (forbid) cursing and violence upon the person being delivered and us; also that there be no harm to the room or its contents. We are children of God and I did NOT want to hear cursing!

In this case with Desiree's back, I was praying in tongues for wisdom on what to do and the thought came to ask the Lord to, "Please send an angel to take this thing out of the area to someplace where the others won't know where it is and can't hurt it."

This may seem like a silly prayer to you, but remember what happened when Jesus told "Legion" to come out of the man with an unclean spirit. The whole account is found in Mark 5:1-20.

"And when He had come out of the boat, immediately there met Him out of the tombs a man with an unclean spirit, who had his dwelling among the tombs; and no one could bind him, not even with chains, because he had often been bound with shackles and chains. And the chains had been pulled apart by him and the shackles broken in pieces; neither could anyone tame him. And always, night and day, he was in the mountains and in the tombs, crying out and cutting himself with stones."

Demons are damned and their certain doom is always before them. Their unholy obsession and aim is to destroy and harm as much of God's creation as possible, and take as many humans to hell with them as they can. They feed on man's misery and fear. Jesus said of their leader, the devil, "The thief comes not except to steal, and to kill, and to destroy." John 10: 10). Back to the account in Luke—

"But when he saw Jesus from afar, he ran and worshipped Him. And he cried out with a loud voice and said, 'What have I to do with You, Jesus, Son of the Most High God? I implore You by God that You do not torment me.'

"For He had said to him, 'Come out of the man, unclean spirit!' Then He asked him, 'What is your name?

"And he answered, saying, 'My name is Legion; for we are many.' *And he begged Him earnestly that He would not send them out of the country.*

"Now a large herd of swine was feeding there near the mountains. And all the demons begged Him, saying, 'Send us to the swine, that we may enter them.' And at once Jesus gave them permission. Then the unclean spirits went out and entered the swine (there were about two thousand); and the herd ran violently down a steep place into the sea, and drowned in the sea.

"Now those who fed the swine fled, and they told it in the city and in the country. And they went out to see what it was that had happened. Then they came to Jesus, and saw the one who had been demon-possessed and had the legion, sitting and clothed and in his right mind. . ."

How wonderful of Jesus to rescue that poor man! But then, that is why our Great Shepherd came. Jesus said, "I have come that they may have life, and that they may have it more abundantly." (John 10: 10). "O, Thank You, Lord, for coming to save us! We praise You!" Call out to Him, dear Reader, if you need help in any way! He will help you.

My reason, however, for telling you this is to illustrate that what the Holy Spirit put in my heart to do about that small demon was very much along the line of what Jesus Himself did, when the unclean spirits begged Him not to send them out of the country, except this one wanted just the opposite!

As soon as I asked the Lord to "Please send an angel to take it someplace else," I "saw" a large angel in a white flowing robe flying away with it. The angel had one arm stretched out in front of him holding it at arm's length by the scruff of its neck. Its legs were drawn up and it looked very much like an ugly little monkey being carried away to an unknown destination.

I described this to Desiree as the Lord showed it then she exclaimed, "Donna, when you prayed for an angel, I saw a big angel walk in the front door." She saw it walk in; I saw it flying away. Praise the Lord! "Jesus Christ is the same, yesterday, today, and forever." (Hebrews 13:8)!

On Sunday *two days later*, Desiree was back at church and sang one of her lively songs! Her back had healed quickly when the assignment was cancelled, and the demon removed. She was out and about her regular activities again. Three or four months later, I got Dr. Eby's book.

After the Lord put Dr. Eby's book into my hands and I read it, I started praising and thanking Abba Daddy every day for healing my back, neck, arm, and shoulder— well, every day I remembered. If I forgot to do it for a time, that burning and aching deep in the muscles would start again and that would remind me! I would immediately start praising and thanking Him until it stopped hurting. It never failed.

The first chance I had one Friday, I told Desiree what the Lord had taught Dr. Eby about praising and thanking God daily for one's healing, his experiment to test it, all of it. She listened to everything I said then startled me by saying, almost angrily, "I don't *have* to thank God every day for my healing! He *knows* I'm thankful."

I was silent just looking at her, perplexed, when the Holy Spirit said "Don't say anything else to her about it," so I never did.

We moved to Texas when Christina was 15. A few months before we moved, I was in the area where Desiree lived and stopped by to see her. Ed had taken us to a different church so I seldom saw her, but we did stay in touch. I knew she had had several more surgeries on her back in the ten years since we had prayed together on Friday nights for nine months. At one point she had *two* metal plates and *eight* screws in her back. Later, due to slippage, the doctors removed one plate and four screws! I hadn't seen her for quite awhile.

It took a long time for her to open the door, but when she did and I saw her, I was shocked. She had been taller than me by several inches, but now she was standing in front of me, peering up into my face! I could look over the top of her head! Can vertebrae be removed? It seemed to me like her rib cage was almost sitting on her hip bones, if that's even possible. Perhaps she was just bent over a lot. It was a poor last memory of her, but I know she's in heaven now with the Lord, rejoicing with other saints.

I've sometimes wondered if her deteriorating condition was affected by her reaction (attitude) when I told her about the revelation the Lord gave to Dr. Eby. I don't know why she was so adamant that she did Not have to thank God every day for her healing. If she had praised and thanked Him daily or at least when she thought of it, I wonder if her healing would have remained.

Somehow, I believe we are accountable for what we know and sometimes God's grace covers us in things we don't know. Scripture does say, "Therefore, to him who knows to do good and does not do it, to him it is sin." (James 4:17). Whether her decision had anything to do with her condition or not, God knows. When she reacted as she did and the Holy Spirit said, "Don't speak to her about this anymore," well, let's just say when I fail to honor and thank Abba Daddy for healing me, it isn't because I *chose* not to, or feel I don't need to—it's simply because I forgot. It seems to me there is a difference. I thank God that His grace is greater than my failings.

"Now one of them, when he saw that he was healed, returned, and with a loud voice glorified God, and fell down on his face at His feet, giving Him thanks. And he was a Samaritan." **(Luke 17: 15-16). Praise the Lord!**

Chapter 13

I Wish I Had Known Then...

"And if the blind leads the blind, both will fall into the ditch."
— Matthew 15:14

Have you ever prayed for something in strong faith, but it didn't happen? Let me tell you of a prayer failure early in my walk in the spirit; I believe it was caused by lack of knowledge. I have wished I could do it over again, but the moment and opportunity are gone. I don't want the same thing to happen to you—that's why I'm sharing this.

The summer after I received the baptism of the Holy Spirit, March 10, 1979, while we were still members of the Church of Christ, the church had a picnic at a park one Sunday afternoon. In attendance was a brother in the church who was out of prison on parole, who was blind.

The promises of Jesus were so real to me that as we sat at a picnic table, I asked him if I could pray for him to receive his sight. I rightly told him, *"Jesus said 'These signs will follow those who believe: In My name they will lay hands on the sick and they will recover,'"* (Mark 16:17–18) and other promises in the Word. He consented.

An elder was nearby and I asked him if he would join us, so we prayed a faith-filled prayer (at least on my part!) asking the Lord to restore the brother's sight, so he could see when he woke up the next morning. I quoted various promises from the word and was so happy and filled with faith. He seemed very hopeful too.

Well, that night I went to bed in great expectation of his seeing the next day, praising God and thanking Him for healing the brother's eyes. I prayed in tongues and fell asleep praising God. Sometime in the night, I woke up praying in tongues. It was strange—discord and heaviness seemed all around me, pressing down on me. Ed was asleep (he had a "wait and see" attitude about the baptism of the Holy Spirit and wasn't aware of my prayer for the brother). I got up, knelt by the bed and began to pray in tongues. The darkness, heaviness, and resistance were strong, and after awhile, I got very sleepy. I wasn't familiar with spiritual warfare then, nor did I understand "opposition and oppression" in the spirit realm. I didn't know what I was praying about in the spirit. It was cold and my eyes were so heavy with sleep that after awhile, I just got back in bed and fell asleep. When I woke up in the morning, though I felt somewhat uneasy about it, the oppression and urgency were gone. I believe the opportunity was too.

That brother did not receive his sight, much to my surprise and bewilderment, but later, after I *grew* in this new walk in the spirit and learned more about spiritual warfare, I believe I understand what was happening that night. I believe that brother's sight had been "recovering" or returning, and Satan was fighting it with all his might with a demon horde from the pit of hell. We know that a demon prince from hell fought an angel of God, holding back an answer to Daniel's prayers for 21 days (Daniel 10: 12–13).

As I learned more about receiving miracles and answers to prayer, I realized the brother had probably been awake that night too in hope and faith, but powers of darkness were fighting his faith, and mine, for the MANIFESTATION of his healing (because the healing had been done two thousand years before) with doubt, unworthiness, wrong beliefs, etc. (fiery darts of the devil), and he needed help to *receive* his miracle. We all need help in great battles.

I believe the Holy Spirit awakened me that night to stand in the gap for him and fight that battle with him in the spirit realm. After all, the prayer had been "my" idea in the first place, or, probably, the Lord's idea.

You know there is a divine timing with the Lord, a moment in time when a door is opened, an opportunity is offered, a great victory is possible. It is a *kyros* moment. Kyros is a Greek word that means the *appointed time* for something. God has set the time. A great step of faith will probably be required, and one needs to move quickly, in faith. I keep thinking of the rich young ruler (Matthew 19:16-22), who came to Jesus and asked Him, *"Good Teacher, what good thing must I do to inherit eternal life?"*

"So Jesus said to him, 'Why do you call Me good? No one is good but One, that is, God. But if you desire to enter into life, keep the commandments.'" They talked about the commandments, and *"The young man said to Him, 'All these things I have kept from my youth. What do I still lack?'*

"Jesus said to him, 'If you want to be perfect, go, sell what you have and give to the poor, and you will have treasure in heaven, and come, follow Me.'"

Think of it! JESUS gave a *personal invitation* to this young man to follow Him! Our Creator, King of Kings, Prince of Peace, the Lord Himself invited this young man to follow Him. That was a *kyros* moment! Who knows (God knows) what plans God had for that young man. He might have become one of the twelve apostles one day, taking Judas's place. Instead, we don't even know his name. I believe he regretted his decision the rest of his life.

Anyway, we'll never know because "when the young man heard that saying (*to sell everything and give to the poor*), he went away sorrowful, for he had great possessions." A *kyros* moment is just that—a moment, an opening in time when all is prepared for a breakthrough. That exact opportunity will not come again.

I believe that day at the park was a *kyros* moment for both me and the man I prayed for, but as we have seen, a *kyros* moment can be lost. It could be Understood, but Refused; or Unrecognized, until later or maybe never, and therefore, Not Received or acted upon. You must seize GOD's moment.

If I had known then, what I know now, I would have prayed in the power of the Holy Spirit until peace came. Peace in prayer means Victory. Also, I would have asked for the *interpretation* of what I was praying in tongues that night-- and I would not have quit!

At that time I was unaware of Paul's instruction about tongues, *"Therefore let him who speaks in a tongue pray that he may interpret. For if I pray in a tongue, my spirit prays, but **my understanding is unfruitful.** What is the result* *then? I will pray with the spirit and I will also pray with the understanding."* (1 Corinthians 14:13-15a).

Since learning the significance (value!) of this scripture, I have asked for the interpretation of what I have prayed in tongues probably thousands of times. We need so much to be instructed in righteousness (knowing the right thing to do—and doing it) and spiritual warfare, so we know what to do in all cases. The Holy Spirit knows what needs to be done, and He will pray it through us if we will just let Him! But I didn't understand what was happening that dark night, and it had a high cost. I believe the consequences were more serious than I ever knew.

That brother was sent back to prison at some point, which meant at the least he broke parole, where he was later stabbed and killed. Who knows how much his faith was affected by his not receiving his sight after a prayer of agreement based on the word of God? God knows.

Also, if that brother had received his sight, Faith "shock waves" would have gone through the church, the community, and the prison. Revival would have come. Instead, I "got tired" and went to sleep—I *quit*. This is another reason I want *you* to STAND, strong in faith, when you have prayed something according to the word of God and the will of God.

"Therefore take up the whole armor of God, that you may be able to withstand in the evil day, and having done all, to stand." (Ephesians 6:13).

I know it was God's will for him to receive his sight. Jesus paid for his healing 2000 years earlier, but there were spiritual forces of darkness fighting against him in this, and I didn't know enough about spiritual warfare to withstand them. Please don't let this happen to you, dear Reader. God is willing where His word is willing.

That was 35 years ago, and I have been in many battles of faith since then and have seen this pattern of resistance happen over and over again. When the answer is very near or one is on the verge of a breakthrough or when there's a "new beginning" or birth of something, the resistance and attack from Satan is strongest. It seems to go to a new level, but now I know this, so now when the battle is very hard, determination strengthens, FAITH rises and with the help of the Holy Spirit, with joy I fight even harder in the Name of the Lord with the Word of God! I praise and thank God for the answer because I know it is near when the opposition is so strong.

"God is gracious, and His loving-kindness endures forever." I asked Him to forgive me for going to sleep that night and not praying it through, and I know He has. The Lord reminded me of Peter, James, and John going to sleep in the Garden of Gethsemane the night of His betrayal. He knows *"The spirit indeed is willing, but the flesh is weak."* (Matthew 26:41). How I thank God for His great grace and manifold (many-faceted) kindness.

However, now I want to ask *you* to forgive those who, as I did in this case, might have prayed for you in times past with "more zeal than knowledge," and thereby hurt you. I have regretted so much not praying it through, but I had to give my failure to God and forgive myself. The brother and I at the time, of course, just "didn't know what happened." He was disappointed I could tell, as was I.

But God is the God of a thousand chances—and more. He will forgive you if you truly ask Him and will give you another opportunity to obey, complete or whatever is needed. Do not give up if you failed at something. Which of us hasn't? Jesus forgave Peter for denying (three times!) that he even knew Him the night of the betrayal, and later, after His resurrection, told him (three times) to *"Feed My sheep."* (John 21:15-17). What a tremendous responsibility and mission He entrusted to Peter.

God has not given up on us because we have encountered situations we didn't understand. He knows what we know and don't know—and He knows the things we don't even know we don't know. He has not given up on us, so don't give up on yourself. Jesus sent precious Holy Spirit to "teach us all things." (John 14:26). He will teach us if we will learn. *"Though the Lord is on high, yet He regards the lowly; but the proud He knows from afar."* (Psalms 138:6). Do not be proud, my friend—be humble and teachable. God regards the lowly. *"The perverse person is an abomination to the Lord, but His secret counsel is with the upright."* (Proverbs 3:32). He can reveal solutions and strategies to you as you quietly wait on Him, lifting up situations and people to Him, asking for wisdom, insight, and help. *"For the Lord gives wisdom; from His mouth come knowledge and understanding."* (Proverbs 2:6). Praise the Lord!

"Finally, my brethren, be strong in the Lord and in the power of His might. Put on the whole armor of God that you may be able to stand against the wiles of the devil, For we do not wrestle against flesh and blood, but against principalities, against powers, against the rulers of the darkness of this age, against spiritual hosts of wickedness in the heavenly places." **(Ephesians 6:10-12). God's Book has answers and contains wisdom.**

CHAPTER 14

UH-OH, HERE COMES TROUBLE

Now there was a man in their synagogue with an unclean spirit. And he cried out, saying, "Let us alone! What have we to do with You, Jesus of Nazareth? Did You come to destroy us? I know who You are—The Holy One of God!"
— Mark 1:23–24

The Lord once told me, "Little hinges open big doors," meaning small, seemingly insignificant acts of obedience can lead to or be the entry to large, far-reaching events. He often uses small things to position us for greater things or to set us up for divine appointments. Here's an example.

When I was a realtor in southern California, one day at the office I picked up the phone to tell another agent I was sending something to her through the office mail, when a clear thought came, *take it to her office*, so I hung up the phone, walked through our very large front office and down a hallway to her spacious, private office.

Her twenty-year old daughter whom I'll call Lisa was sitting at a desk inside the door. I had spoken to mother and daughter separately about the Lord previously, and both had assured me they were believers.

She said her mom and the rest of the team had gone to lunch. The other times I had been in that office, there had been four to seven people there; today there were just the two of us.

After giving her the paper, I smiled, thanked her, and moved to go when suddenly she blurted out, "I went to a psychic on Saturday!"

"Oh no!" was my instant reaction.

The whole story poured out then—"I went to Arizona with a friend last weekend. She knew about a psychic in the desert and wanted us to go see him. I didn't want to, but she kept asking, so finally I took her, and I went in too." Her eyes got big, "He told me I was going to get married when I was twenty-two, and I'd be pregnant at my wedding, but the father wasn't going to be my fiancé." She and her long-time boyfriend had recently become engaged.

"There's something else; when I walked in and he saw me, he said 'Uh-oh, here comes trouble!' Why did he say that?" She paused as if remembering, then added, "It was really weird there; I felt funny. I didn't like it and wanted to leave, but she didn't. When we finally got outside, I jumped in my car, locked the doors and drove home as fast as I could! I was afraid; it felt like something was following me. When I got to my apartment, I turned on all the lights and slept with them on. I'm afraid to be in my apartment alone now, and I'm leaving all the lights on."

I wanted to make sure I had understood her correctly. "You mean all the lights in your apartment are on right now?"

Sadly she nodded, "So I don't have to come home to a dark apartment."

At that moment, the Holy Spirit showed me this was a cry for help. She was afraid; she was asking me what she should do.

"Oh Lisa, you're a child of God, but you walked right into the devil's territory! No wonder the guy said, 'Uh-oh, here comes trouble' when he saw you. You probably had two big angels with you, one on each side. He probably could see them because the demons showed him.

"You opened a door to the devil by going there. You felt like something was following you because it was. Because you went there of your own free will, it gave the demons a *legal right* to attach to you, and the angels couldn't prevent it. But God loves you; I think that's why He sent me here today, and arranged for no one else to be here--to help you.

"Lisa, you're God's precious little lamb; Jesus died for you. By going there it was like you were saying, *Jesus wasn't good enough*, that He was withholding something good from you-- knowledge of the future. You were insulting the Lord by this, Lisa, though I know you didn't mean it that way. God has hidden the future from us because that's best, but you sought *from the devil* knowledge that God has hidden. And what a future he made up for you! Look at how much harm he did in one visit. But that's not GOD's plan for you. The devil is a liar—and so are his demons." She was listening intently.

Gently, I said, "Lisa, you need to repent and tell God you're sorry you went to a psychic, and ask Him to forgive you."

Precious Lisa prayed that day in her mother's office and asked God to forgive her for what she had done. *"If we confess our sins, He is faithful and just to forgive us our sins and to cleanse us from all unrighteousness."* (I John 1:9), praise God. She renounced all agreement with Satan and his demons and declared that JESUS is her Lord and that she *chose* to serve Him only. It was beautiful.

Then in JESUS' Name, we commanded the demon(s) to leave her and her home. We put the protection of the *blood of Jesus* over her, her apartment, car, and belongings. I told her to anoint her apartment when she got home and dedicate it to the Lord. She was so relieved and thankful and *wasn't afraid* anymore! Hallelujah! That's what Jesus will do for you.

That night at home, I wrote a letter to Lisa giving her some scriptures about this. I made a copy for myself and still have it. Here are two of the scriptures: *"Give no regard to mediums and familiar spirits; do not seek after them, to be defiled by them. I am the Lord."* (Leviticus18:19).

And *"There shall not be found among you anyone who makes his son or daughter pass through the fire (a heinous method of child sacrifice), or one who practices witchcraft, or a soothsayer (fortune teller), or one who interprets omens, or a sorcerer, or who conjures up spells, or a medium (one who invites demons to speak through him/her), or a spiritist, or one who calls up the dead. For all who do these things are an abomination to the Lord."* (Deuteronomy 18:10-12a).

Please note: If a child of God goes to a psychic, besides leaving the paths of righteousness, it also gives opportunity to Satan to taunt and mock God about him/her coming to *him* for guidance or information. If you have done this, please repent and ask for forgiveness. Remember, when David sinned with Bathsheba, then had her husband, Uriah, killed to cover up his sin? Nathan, the prophet, was sent by God to David, and among other things said *"because of this deed you have given great occasion to the enemies of the Lord to blaspheme."* (2 Samuel 12:14a). According to Cruden's Complete Concordance, blaspheme is *"to revile or curse God. . . It means intentional indignity offered to God or sacred things."*

And remember Job: *"Now there was a day when the sons of God came to present themselves before the Lord, and Satan also came among them. Then the Lord said to Satan, 'Have you considered My servant Job, that there is none like him on the earth, a blameless and upright man, one who fears God and shuns evil?'*

"So Satan answered the Lord and said, 'Does Job fear God for nothing? Have You not made a hedge around him, around his household, and around all that he has on every side? You have blessed the work of his hands, and his possessions have increased in the land. But now, stretch out Your hand and touch all that he has, and he will surely curse You to Your face!'" (Job1:1–8).

Do you see Satan's evil intent in this? Job was the Best of all mankind in his lifetime, and Satan told God that Job only served Him because He blessed him. In other words, *no one* on earth loved God for Himself! Satan was trying to hurt God; he accuses us to God and accuses GOD to us. He and his minions are always trying to deceive and discourage people, to make them doubt God's kindness, goodness, and love.

His name means "the adversary" or "the enemy." Jesus said of him, *"He was a murderer from the beginning and does not stand in the truth, because there is no truth in him. When he speaks a lie, he speaks from his own resources, for he is a liar and the father of it."* (John 8:44b).

And he was lying then; Job did love God, no matter what happened. One of the greatest statements of faith in the Bible was made by Job *after* the calamities Satan caused, including the death of *all ten of Job's children* in one day! Job still said of God, *"Though He slay me, yet will I trust Him."* (Job 13:15). Isn't that beautiful? May we have this same faith that God is good and trust Him no matter what happens.

"Be sober, be vigilant, because your adversary the devil walks about like a roaring lion, seeking whom he may devour. Resist him, steadfast in the faith, knowing that the same sufferings are experienced by your brotherhood in the world." **(I Peter 5:8–9).**

Chapter 15

There's Something In My Closet

For He said to him, "Come out of the man, unclean spirit!" Then He asked him "What is your name?" And he Answered saying, "My name is Legion; for we are many."
— Mark 5:8–9

In what I'm going to share now, I want you to be aware that once demons have right of entry into a place, they will not leave just because the person or group that gave them entry leaves or even dies. Yes, some will go with him or her, but some remain, and others come, even when the "host" is gone. Haunted houses are where occult activities, murder, violence, suicide, great trauma, sexual sin, etc. have taken place and demonic spirits have remained. BUT *"greater is HE that is in us than he that is in the world!"* (I John 4:4). The Lord has given *us* the authority to Cast Them Out! Now, I want to honor someone whose book shed light on this subject for me back in the 1980s.

What I was beginning to suspect along this line was powerfully confirmed through George Otis' inspiring book, *High Adventure.* In it, George shares about his and his wife's search for a larger house to accommodate the growing Bible study they hosted in their southern California home.

Their realtor took them to a huge, overgrown, abandoned property, once considered *the* party house for Hollywood's famous and infamous. George said he was immediately "repulsed by its dark atmosphere."

He wrote, "No wonder the hairs along my arms were raised as I walked through the place! It may have been haunted from depraved spirits of iniquity. It was as if they remained from past affairs." It was God's house for them though, and eventually, they acquired ownership.

That was when George put into action a plan or remedy (strategy) God had given him. Before they moved in, he brought Bible tapes, a repeating tape recorder, and big speakers, which he set up in the center of the house and left running at high volume day and night for a period of time. "Every atom in that house heard His Word...as well as every evil angel, too. The place came under the thunder and cleansing power of it! The whole atmosphere of the sour old place suddenly turned sweet. The place was clean and clear and full of light at last!" Hallelujah! Child of God, that still works today!

Dear Reader, one generation teaches another. We can learn so much from those who have gone before us. *"That which has been is what will be. That which is done is what will be done. And there is nothing new under the sun. Is there anything of which it may be said, 'See, this is new'? It has already been done in ancient times before us."* (Ecclesiastes 1:9–10). When the need arises, I do what George did, and other times I cleanse places by anointing them with oil in Jesus' name and *commanding* the demons to leave. Here is an example.

One day our younger son, Torrey, who was eleven at the time, came to me and said, "There's something in my closet."

Since I had anointed numerous places that had "resident demons" and had seen wonderful victory for the people who lived in these homes, I knew it was very possible and immediately believed him. "Oh, there is, is there? Well, we'll just take care of that!"

He nodded, "Yes, it comes out at night. Sometimes it's under the bed and tries to scare me." Also, sometimes at night he would be sitting at his desk doing homework; everything would be very quiet, when suddenly he would sense it was there. He would get goose bumps; then his radio would quietly come on by itself.

You don't need to be afraid of things like this, dear Reader. We do not deal with these things in our own name, wisdom, or strength; they are done, and won, in the name of JESUS, our Lord and Savior! Hallelujah!

We lived in a three-bedroom townhouse in southern California at the time; all the bedrooms were upstairs. Torrey went upstairs while I got my little bottle of anointing oil from my purse; then I joined him. He was waiting in the hallway outside his bedroom door.

With him watching and agreeing with me in prayer, I anointed above the door and both sides of the doorframe based on Exodus 12:22a–23b. *"And you shall take a bunch of hyssop, dip it in the blood that is in the basin, and strike the lintel and two doorposts with the blood that is in the basin…and when He sees the blood on the lintel and on the two doorposts, the Lord will pass over the door and not allow the destroyer to come into your houses to strike you."* We used oil for this, representing the blood of Jesus.

The blood referred to in this verse is that of a Passover lamb. One per household was offered annually in Israel for many centuries before Jesus walked on earth. The killing of the Passover lamb foreshadowed the Lord's death on the cross where He would die for our sins. Jesus is the Lamb of God. John the Baptist received this revelation. *"The next day John saw Jesus coming toward him, and said, 'Behold the Lamb of God who takes away the sin of the world!'"* (John 1:35–36). Praise the Lord!

Anointing the door with the lamb's blood was also a picture of the *blood of Jesus* being applied to the door of our hearts and lives when we receive Him as our Lord and Savior, praise God!

When I anoint a house, room, or business, I usually address, "Every spirit in this room (house or business) that does not *willingly* bend the knee and *joyfully* proclaim 'Jesus is Lord,' I command you to leave here now. Go to the pit and stay there, in Jesus' holy and mighty Name!"

Philippians 2:10–11a tells us, *"that at the name of Jesus every knee should bow of those in heaven, and those on earth* (that's us), *and those under the earth* (in hell), *and that every tongue should confess that Jesus Christ is Lord."* Jesus told us, *"When an unclean spirit goes out of a man, he goes through dry places, seeking rest and finds none."* (Matthew 12:43). I can't think of any place dryer than a pit in hell! My command is based on these and other scriptures.

We went into Torrey's room, which contained his bunk bed, dresser and small desk, and I was going to command it to leave, but a thought came to me about

Jesus *asking the name of the demon in the man with an unclean spirit, who lived in the tombs.* That's the scripture at the beginning of this chapter and also referred to in Chapter 12. The full account is found in Mark 5:1–20. It is a wonderful story of the power and kindness of our dear Lord.

I didn't care about its name, but I did want something else. I DO NOT recommend doing this unless the Holy Spirit gives you permission. It is not a game. Maybe the Lord put it in my heart because He knew I'd write about it one day, and He wanted to demonstrate that these things are real, but HIS POWER is mightier!

I didn't like that that thing had been hiding, scaring my son, and I wanted to force it to do something before it left, so *Torrey could see* that *Jesus gave us authority "over all the power of the enemy."* (Luke 10:19). I had never done this before, and never have since, but that one time only, I said, "Before you go, I command you in Jesus' name—to manifest or reveal yourself. You have to reveal yourself, but with NO VIOLENCE, and in a way that is Not Harmful and Not Scary. You must reveal yourself, and then GO—in Jesus' name!"

His bedroom had a sliding door with vertical blinds that opened onto a small balcony. The room was perfectly still; the sliding door was shut, the air conditioning off. When I commanded it, in Jesus' name, to reveal itself, suddenly ONE vertical blind began to vibrate, clicking against the one on each side—which did not move. It vibrated evenly, the whole thing, top and bottom: no swing, no sway, just a precise vibration, the third one from the latch.

Torrey said I shouted, "There it is! Praise the Lord!" I do remember shouting, "There it is!" striding to the glass door, sliding it back, and strongly saying, "Now go to the pit, in JESUS' name, and never come back!" The vibrating abruptly stopped, the demon left, and Torrey was never bothered again. He wasn't afraid anymore either, praise God.

So why am I telling you this? My point is that "unclean spirits" as Jesus called them, can be in a house, a building, on a piece of land or even on individual objects because of things that have happened there or curses that have been deliberately set on them.

One time, I was anointing or doing a "spiritual housecleaning" in a house where the woman, a believer with a drinking problem and not knowledgeable in the word, was having real difficulties, and I felt led to open the entry-closet door (unusual), and when I did, I "saw" in the spirit a little blonde girl, maybe 4 years old, crouched there, terrified. This was a "word of knowledge" (1 Corinthians 12:8), one of the nine gifts of the Holy Spirit, operating. He was showing me what had gone on in that house, so I would know what strongholds were there, and therefore, what needed to be done.

I described to the woman what I was seeing. With fear (I believe it was the fear of the Lord God who reveals secret things, Daniel 2:28), she said the neighbors had told her that a little blonde-headed girl had lived there before, who was being abused. She was poorly cared for and they could hear shouting, crying and screaming at times. I don't know if any of them did anything about it, but I knew the evil spirits remaining there would try to influence or affect anyone else who lived in that house. Among other things, the woman had been having nightmares—which could have been from a spirit of fear. In Jesus' mighty name, I commanded spirits of fear, terror, child abuse, anger, rage, etc. to leave that house! The whole atmosphere changed after the house and property were anointed.

When you are doing a "spiritual housecleaning," ask the Lord for discernment on what needs to be done. The Holy Spirit can show you through the gift of "discerning of spirits" (1 Corinthians 12:10), or a "word of knowledge," or "word of wisdom" as He showed me.

Note: I have prayed for that little girl, a grown woman by now, wherever she is that God would protect and help her. Our prayers can be used by God to put protection, provision, etc. over people, even though we do not know them by name. God knows them.

I recommend you anoint your home to clear it of any unclean spirits that may be there because of previous occupants or activities.

One other thing for this chapter: if a child tells you there's something in his/her room, or that he's afraid to be in his room by himself, or afraid to go to sleep at night, please take it seriously. It is wonderful to pray with the child and ask God to set angels around him to protect him as he sleeps, and you should do this—BUT you should also Clear the Room! A simple illustration would be setting lovely flowers with a "heavenly" fragrance around a room, but leaving a stinkpot under the bed! Praying for the good is good, but you also need to get rid of the bad.

Here is another instance. About two years ago, I was invited to speak to the Women's Ministry of a local church, and a woman came up to me before I spoke and told me she and her husband had heard me speak on spiritual warfare about eight months earlier. Their five or six-year old daughter had been having nightmares every night and hearing voices and noises they didn't hear. Their thirteen-year old son had begun to hear the voices, but not the noises. After hearing me speak on this subject, they went home and anointed their home and property *that night.* The nightmares, voices, and noises stopped that night. Praise the Lord! He has given us authority to deal with these things; many believers just need teaching and instruction about this.

You know, dear Reader, anointing a property can be done quietly without shouting or fanfare. Speak confidently with faith that, in Jesus' name, it is happening. It might sound fanciful, but to me the homes and land actually look cleaner, more beautiful and peaceful afterwards (after all, demons are called *unclean* spirits). The lamps seem to give a brighter glow and even sunlight outside seems brighter and clearer.

Ask the Holy Spirit to guide you on whether you need to do this or not. I believe lands, properties, and animals want to be cleansed and blessed. Animals can be traumatized, terrified, abused, and abandoned. They too benefit from being prayed for and even anointed in the name of Jesus for healing and blessing.

"Then the seventy returned with joy, saying, 'Lord, even the demons are subject to us in Your name.' And He said to them, 'I saw Satan fall like lightning from heaven. Behold, I give you the authority to trample on serpents and scorpions, and over all the power of the enemy, and nothing shall by any means hurt you. Nevertheless do not rejoice in this, that the spirits are subject to you, but rather rejoice because your names are written in heaven'" **(Luke 10:17–20). "Yes, Lord! And Thank You!!"**

Chapter 16

Your Wife Can Use This Too

Who ever goes to war at his own expense? Who plants a vineyard and does not eat of its fruit? Or who tends a flock and does not drink of the milk of the flock?

— 1 Corinthians 9:7

One Sunday morning in August, 1989, Ed and I with our two youngest children, Torrey and Christina, were rushing to the American Airlines ticket counter at Ontario Airport in southern California to pick up his ticket for a business flight to Chicago. We had to miss church to get him there on time for his 11 a.m. flight.

To our surprise, there was a long line of people ahead of us with bags, boxes, and suitcases scattered about them. As we inched forward, I was praying Ed would make the plane on time, but it turned out God had a different plan. *"A man's steps are ordered of the Lord; how then can a man understand his own way?"* (Proverbs 20:24).

The moment we reached the counter, the door behind it opened, a man stepped out, walked over to us and said,

"We are overbooked on this flight at 11 a. m. If you will wait for the 1:15 p.m. flight, we will give you a voucher for $200, good for any flight with American Airlines. What do you say, sir?" The man glanced from Ed to me; Ed and I looked at each other and both nodded yes.

As the man was filling out the voucher, he paused, lifted his head, looked straight at me and said, "Your wife can use this too."

As we walked away, Ed held out the voucher to me, "Here, you take it and use it." This was his second business trip in a few months while I was home with our two youngest children, who were 6 and 2. Our two older daughters were married, and Paul, our older son, was in college. Torrey and Christina are our two late blessings; I was 38 and 42, respectively, when they were born. I think Ed wanted to give me a vacation!

I accepted the voucher and said, "Thank you! The Lord has a purpose for this; He'll show me what it is."

Before we went to the waiting area with Ed, I found a pay phone and called Jeannie, a friend from church, who had called me the week before saying she wanted to talk to me about something. We had agreed to meet for lunch on Sunday after Ed left, so I called her, and we adjusted the time. Later at the restaurant, Jeannie shared the following:

"Donna, I was born and raised in Florida. I go back there every summer for a visit; I just went in July. You know Larry Lea's having the Miami Prayer Breakthrough in November?" I nodded.

Larry Lea was pastor of Church on the Rock in Rockwell, Texas. At one time, this anointed young preacher had been youth pastor at Beverly Hills Baptist Church in Dallas, where the youth department rose from 40 to 1,000 under his leadership. In 1980 he was invited to pastor the small Church on the Rock, which consisted of 12 people! Within five years, it had grown to over 5,000. I believe the secret of this growth was prayer. Larry Lea is a man of prayer.

He began to be invited to other churches to share the things God was teaching him about prayer, especially the Lord's Prayer, holding Prayer Clinics, then Prayer Rallies. Later the Lord instructed him to hold three-day Prayer Breakthroughs in 21 major American cities to pray for those cities and their surrounding areas.

The first one, the Los Angeles Prayer Breakthrough, was held in Anaheim, CA, in June, 1989. Our home church chartered two buses to take people to it; Irlene and I went on one of the buses. I was blessed to attend the first four of those Breakthroughs; Irlene and I had the privilege of attending three of them together.

On the last night of the L. A. Prayer Breakthrough, Larry told us the next Breakthrough would be in Miami in November. He said, "Ask the Lord what significant contribution you can make to the Miami Prayer Breakthrough." This was the beginning of a series of amazing events for me.

We had been a one-income family since before Christina's birth, and finances were tight, but I obediently, silently, asked, *"Lord, what significant contribution can I make to the Miami Prayer Breakthrough?"*

Just like that, in my spirit, I heard *"Your prayers are a significant contribution to the Miami Prayer Breakthrough."* I was speechless, and very humbled, thinking about what the Holy Spirit had said. After a time, I said, *"Thank You, Lord. Well, I certainly can pray for Miami and the Breakthrough from home."* I had no expectation of being there in person. About two months had passed since then, and now I was sitting in a restaurant with my two youngest children listening to Jeannie.

She continued, "Well, on the plane coming home, the Lord told me I have a spiritual heritage in Florida, and I have spiritual authority there because I was born there. He told me to go to the Miami Prayer Breakthrough.

"I told Him I would, but I asked if one other woman could go with me. I've been praying and praying, asking Him who it should be. Last week He told me it was you–you should go. Donna, will you go to the Miami Prayer Breakthrough with me in November?"

This was about two hours after I had received the voucher! With sudden understanding, I responded, "Yes, I'll go. And Jeannie, I think the Lord just gave me the plane fare." I pulled out the voucher and showed it to her, explaining how I had just gotten it. We were rejoicing and praising the Lord through that meal!

We also prayed about the plane fare, and I asked the Lord for a *"super-duper airline special so that I, and every person appointed by Him* to go to Florida for the Prayer Breakthrough, could go!

Well, just a week or two later at Saturday early-morning prayer at church, Jeannie asked me, "Did you see American Airline's special? Just $198 roundtrip anywhere in the continental United States! I got my ticket." She told me the special had just ended on Friday, the day before, at noon!

No, I hadn't seen it! When I got home, I called American Airlines; the roundtrip from southern California to Florida was over $350 now! I felt so bad; God had given me a *"super-duper airline special,"* and I had missed it.

I apologized to the Lord and told Him I was so sorry about missing His wonderful special; I just hadn't expected it so soon! The Prayer Breakthrough wasn't until November. I guess I hadn't expected the special until October. I asked Him to "Please forgive me and give me another special. I promise to call every week to see if they have another special."

It was on my first call at the end of the next week, that I was told, "We have a special to Florida right now—$262 roundtrip." I booked a spot immediately on the same flight with Jeannie.

So, God's Best for me on the airfare was $198 ($2 less than the voucher); His second best was $262. As stated earlier, there is a timing, a window of opportunity for God's Best…but God is very merciful.

A few days later, Irlene told me God had told *her* to pay the extra $62 for my ticket AND buy me some new clothes for the trip! She took me shopping, and I picked out several nice outfits. ("Thank You, Lord, for Irlene who was such a blessing in my life and went home to You in 1998.")

Finally, the day came when Jeannie and I got on the plane headed to Florida for the Miami Prayer Breakthrough.

***"As they ministered to the Lord and fasted, the Holy Spirit said, 'Now separate to me Barnabas and Saul for the work to which I have called them.'"* (Acts 13:2). God still does this today!**

Chapter 17

Jeannie, Get Your Anointing Oil!

For we do not wrestle against flesh and blood,
but against principalities, Against powers,
against the rulers of the darkness of this age,
against Spiritual hosts of wickedness in
the heavenly places.
— Ephesians 6:12

The only time I've ever actually seen a demon with my own eyes was on this trip. It was standing a few feet from me, glaring at me. I'll tell you about it in due time. To continue, Jeannie and I spent the first night at her parents' home. The next day, her father dropped us off at a car rental agency where he had graciously arranged and paid for a car for our use, since it was a four-hour drive to Miami from there.

A little side note: Jeannie was and still is a Mary Kay consultant and had received a beautiful red Grand AM shortly before our trip. To her surprise, the agency had a red Grand AM set aside for us, just like her car at home!

She had been wishing she could show her family what her new Mary Kay car looked like. This small detail is another proof to me of God's love and intimate knowledge of us, how specific and custom-tailored His blessings are. *"Delight yourself also in the Lord and He shall give you the desires of your heart."* (Psalms 37:4). Praise the Lord!

Jeannie had arranged for us to stay with two of her former high school classmates, married and living in West Palm Beach area about 80 miles north of Miami. We ate dinner with them only the first night because we were at the Breakthrough the following three nights. The wife was a self-avowed atheist, her husband an agnostic. She told us bluntly at dinner that first night, "I don't want you talking about God!" There was a stack of Playboy magazines in the guest bathroom, which they made no effort to hide or remove.

Larry started the Prayer Breakthroughs at 7:14 p.m., a reminder of the promise in 2 Chronicles 7:14, *"If My people who are called by My name will humble themselves, and pray and seek My face, and turn from their wicked ways, then I will hear from heaven, and will forgive their sin and heal their land."* Child of God, the condition of our nation depends on us! God is faithful and He will do His part if we will do ours.

The Prayer Breakthrough was powerful! The music and worship were glorious and the prayers awesome. By the time it ended each night and Jeannie and I drove 80 miles, it was close to 1 a.m. before we got to our hosts' home. They had loaned Jeanne a key for us to get in, and they left for work before we were up in the mornings.

Well, on Friday morning, Jeannie and I were sitting in the comfortable room off the kitchen overlooking their beautiful backyard that ran down to a canal. We were quietly reading our Bibles and sipping coffee, when I "happened" to glance over to the kitchen and SAW a demon standing there glaring at me! This is the only time I have ever seen a demon with my natural eyes. This was the "discerning of spirits," one of the nine gifts of the Holy Spirit operating (1 Corinthians 12:7–11).

It was about six feet tall with light gray skin, wearing black pantaloons, was bare–chested with wide metallic bracelets on its upper and lower arms. It had black hair and, believe it or not, pointed ears. It had long, 3 to 4–inch finger nails, and its hands were clenched at its sides. It was glaring at me with fury, and in my spirit I heard it say, "GET OUT! This is *my* house and these are *my* people!"

As soon as I saw and heard it, it knew it had been exposed and disappeared or, more likely, the Holy Spirit had shown me all I needed to know. I sprang up, grabbed my open Bible, hugged it to my chest, and RAN to the kitchen, yelling, "Jeannie, get your anointing oil!"

I ran to the exact spot where it had been standing, and with Bible against my chest and one arm stretched towards heaven, I shouted, "This is NOT your house and these are NOT your people! Jesus created them. You did not shed any blood for these people; you didn't give one drop of blood for them. JESUS did! Jesus gave *His blood for them; He died for them!* Jesus wants them and He's going to have them!! We bind you in Jesus' Name. You leave this house and you leave these people—in Jesus' mighty Name!"

Though I didn't think about it at the time, spirits don't have blood. That's part of the reason Jesus had to come as a man though He is God, so He could die for us. *"But Christ came as High Priest... Not with the blood of goats and calves, but with His own blood He entered the Most Holy Place once for all, having obtained eternal redemption. ...so Christ was offered once to bear the sins of many."* (Hebrews 9:11–12).

Also after the resurrection, when He appeared to the apostles in His resurrected body, Jesus told us something about spirits:

"Now as they said these things, Jesus Himself stood in the midst of them, and said to them, 'Peace to you.' But they were terrified and supposed they had seen a spirit.

"And He said to them, 'Why are you troubled? And why do doubts arise in your hearts? Behold My hands and My feet, that it is I Myself. Handle Me and see, for ***a spirit does not have flesh and bone as you see I have.*** *When he had said this, He showed them His hands and His feet."* (Luke 24:36–40). If spirits don't have flesh and bone, they don't have blood either.

Jeannie and I anointed the house except for the master bedroom. I believe our Heavenly Father sent us to their home to talk with them, explain the gospel and give them a chance to receive Jesus, but we were told the first night in strong and definite terms not to talk about God. So, though we anointed the house, the demon probably remained. If a person chooses not to receive Jesus and not to repent, demons can legally stay. Sadly, the husband died a few years ago of alcohol–related diseases.

The last night of the Breakthrough was awesome and ended gloriously on a high note. We had sat in the balcony on the right each night and at the end, I went down to the main floor to mingle. One of Larry's staff members and I started talking, and I told her about the voucher and my coming to Florida with Jeannie. She studied me for a moment, then said, "You should come to the Chicago Prayer Breakthrough next April."

"Well, let's pray," I said, and we did. I asked the Lord that if it were His will for me to go to Chicago, that when I asked Irlene about our going together, she would say 'Great!'" Then while the other woman prayed, I "saw" Irlene and myself on a plane fastening our seatbelts, and the plane lifted off.

Jeanne and I had a wonderful trip. We saw various members of her family and prayed with several of them. After we got back to California, I called Irlene and told her about our trip and about seeing the demon in the people's house; then I said, "I think you and I are supposed to go to Chicago for the Chicago Prayer Breakthrough in April."

She responded, "Great!" So it was settled—we would be going to Chicago in April. The Lord had shown us His will.

"But even if our gospel is veiled, it is veiled to those who are perishing, whose minds the god of this age has blinded, who do not believe, lest the light of the gospel of the glory of Christ, who is in the image of God, should shine on them. For we do not preach ourselves, but Christ Jesus the Lord." **(2 Corinthians 4:3–5).**

Chapter 18

LORD, I Ask for a Double Portion!

And so it was, when they had crossed over,
that Elijah said to Elisha, "Ask! What may I do
for you before I am taken away from you?"
And Elisha said, "Please let a double portion
of Your spirit be upon me."
— II Kings 2:9

God doesn't show you everything when He gives you a glimpse of a future event. He just shows you what you need to know, to know His will or to comfort and strengthen you in what you're going through or praying about. This was the case with the picture He had given me of Irlene and I on a plane taking off for Chicago. I didn't know that when that time came, I would look like I had been hit in the face with a battering ram.

For several weeks before we left, the Lord had led me to pray for and minister to a woman in our church who was dying. I wrote about it in my first book, calling her "Shirley." It was quite a battle for her soul, and in the course of it near the end, the devil tried to kill me one night on the way to her house by having a young man cross into my lane, aim his car directly at mine, and hit me full speed in a head-on collision.

BUT, praise God, despite my deep bruises and sore muscles, by God's grace "none of my bones were broken!" Also by the grace of God, Irlene and I did go to Chicago right on schedule, though I looked like I'd been in a fight with a prize fighter. Hallelujah anyway! Irlene and I did everything the Lord had shown us we were to do while in Chicago; we rented a car, drove to a certain place, and did a spiritual cleansing there and some other things, as well as joining about 6,800 other believers each night in a powerful, anointed prayer gathering. We returned to California with joy, looking forward to the San Francisco Prayer Breakthrough in the fall. By that time, thankfully, my swollen face, black eye, and visible bruises had healed.

We decided to use my car for the trip to San Francisco. I believe it was because Irlene had a red 1957 Mustang with white leather seats, her "baby," and she didn't want to drive it up there. I had purchased another car to replace the one that had been "totaled" when Satan tried to kill me, with part of the small insurance settlement I had received. (Of course, I tithed and gave offerings from it first.)

In preparation for the trip, the Saturday before we left I took my car to a shop for a lube job and tune up and at their recommendation, I also purchased two new tires which they mounted. Another woman, Irene, whom Irlene had met when they were both answering prayer–line phones at TBN in Santa Ana, wanted to go with us, so there were three of us who started out for San

Francisco that beautiful day, early Wednesday morning, October 31, 1990.

We made good time through L. A., but while going up the grapevine, a stretch of highway going over the Tehachapi Mountains, the car started to overheat. I pulled off at a place provided for this. The first man to stop *insisted* I rev the engine, and it would cool off. To make a long story short, after the engine burst and other men stopped, rushed to lift the hood off the smoking, steaming engine and declared it ruined, he seemed suddenly awake. He lowered his head, hunched his shoulders, met my eyes one time with a furtive look, then quietly, but quickly, slunk back to his truck, hopped in, and took off.

While I waited with the car, Irlene and Irene were given a ride to Bakersfield where Irlene called her AAA service. A tow truck eventually arrived, and the car and I finally made it to the garage in Bakersfield where they were waiting. By this time, we were all hungry for lunch. The people at the garage said they would keep the car until we returned. The head gasket was blown, and the block cracked. Irlene made arrangements to rent a car. By the time we secured a car, transferred our luggage, ate lunch, and got back on the road with Irlene driving this time—we had lost *five* hours!

As evening fell and we approached San Jose, where we were going to stay with a family who were former members of our home church in Walnut, CA, we heard on the radio the Prayer Breakthrough had begun. It almost caused a riot.

This Breakthrough was unlike any of the others, in the events surrounding it and the press coverage leading up to it. A group of ministers had announced a march of Christians on *Halloween night* through the Castro District, the stronghold of homosexual and lesbian activity in the city. This caused outrage and a tremendous backlash. At the advice of police and local pastors, the march was cancelled, but the damage had been done. The ire and rage of many of the inhabitants of the Castro District and other groups had been raised. But God had a plan as you will see.

In the morning of the first day of the Breakthrough, Eric Pryor, Wiccan high priest of New Earth Temple in San Francisco, and Dr. Dick Bernal, pastor of Jubilee Christian Center in San Jose, were both on a local television show, "People Are Talking," discussing the three-day Prayer Breakthrough, which was starting that night. Pryor was under the impression that the Breakthrough was aimed at condemning homosexuals. Pastor Bernal wisely used this opportunity to explain about spiritual warfare against territorial spirits, not people.

Afterwards, he invited Eric to lunch. During lunch, he invited him to the Breakthrough that night to hear for himself that Larry Lea was not preaching hate, and the Breakthrough was not about being at war with certain groups of people. Eric agreed to come to the meeting to see what it was about, but that afternoon with 30 of his followers, the Wiccan High Priest performed a public and highly publicized, ritualistic cursing of Larry and those who would be attending the Breakthrough that night. This was covered by both local and national media, but we didn't know anything about all this as we were trying to get *to* San Francisco that day.

That evening, unbeknownst to anyone else, before he and his fiancée left for the Breakthrough, Eric secretly concealed a small *handgun* in his boot, resolved to shoot Larry Lea if he spoke against homosexuals!

Here is a newspaper article about some of the events of that night. This was published November 2, 1990, by Times Staff Writer, Mark A. Stein:

> *"The Rev. Larry Lea sought to 'exorcise sin' from San Francisco on Wednesday night, but had to do it from inside the Civic Center Auditorium while 1,500 vocal demonstrators chanted outside and San Francisco engaged in usual raucous and lascivious Halloween festivities...*
>
> *The demonstration was nasty—the primarily gay and lesbian protesters chanted, "Bring back the lions!" as the Christians entered the ornate hall—but relatively peaceful. Most of the demonstrators including pagans, simply shouted, 'Go home!'"*

Another account said there were three thousand protesters and reported that a bus filled with Christians was surrounded by protesters such that the Christians were unable to disembark until police escorted them to the building. The next night, a woman who had been on that bus told me the police formed a sort of "passageway" for the believers to go through. "People were shoving, pushing, and shouting at us. Some people reached out and tried to grab me as we were trying to get to the building, but the policeman pulled me loose and sort of pushed me towards the door!"

I didn't know any of this while it was happening, but I was so disappointed we were missing the first night of the Breakthrough that, sitting in the backseat of the car in the dark as we neared San Jose, I cried out loud to God,

"Abba Daddy, the devil made us miss this first night, but I'm asking for a Double Portion of the battle tomorrow night—in fact, for the next *two* nights, to make up for not being there tonight! In JESUS' name, I ask this!"

***"Now before they lay down, the men of Sodom, both old and young, all the people from every quarter, surrounded the house ... Then they said, 'This one came in to sojourn, and he keeps acting as a judge ...' So they pressed against the man Lot, and came near to break down the door. But the men reached out their hands and pulled Lot into the house with them and shut the door."* (Genesis 19:4, 9–10).**

Chapter 19

There He Is! That's the Witch!

But there was a certain man called Simon, who previously practiced sorcery in the city and astonished the people of Samaria...to whom they all gave heed, from the least to the greatest... and they heeded him because he had astonished them with his sorceries for a long time.

— Acts 8:9–11

Thursday evening we arrived at the Civic Center in good time and were seated up in the balcony on the right, halfway back. There was excitement, energy, and expectation in the air. Everyone was buzzing!

The lady beside me leaned against me and loudly whispered (so I could hear her!), "There he is! That's the witch down there!" and pointed to the main level where a group of men were standing in front of the first row, between the first row and the stage.

"That's him! He's a witch—the one in black."

I turned to look at her, "What?!" She repeated her message, pointing at him.

"You mean a warlock?" I asked.

"Yes!"

I saw him then. He did stand out, dressed in black from head to toe. As I sat there watching from my perch quite a ways from him, I remembered the little magazine in my purse. The day before as we had been standing around waiting in Bakersfield, Irene, who had come with Irlene and me, had given copies of *Voice* magazine to several people we met along the way.

Voice is a wonderful, small–sized, maybe 5" x 7" magazine published by Full Gospel Businessmen's Fellowship International. It is full of powerful testimonies of men who have had their lives changed by coming to Jesus. She told me she bought back issues in bulk to hand out.

I had had a sudden, strong desire to give one and had asked if I could have one copy to give. She handed me one, and I had held it between both hands and prayed out loud, "Lord, please let me give this little magazine to Someone Special! Someone who will receive it and read it, time and time again, and Receive the Truth that is in it! We pull down prejudices and every high thing that exults itself against the knowledge of God regarding this! Thank You, Abba Daddy, in Jesus' name!" Later, in the car, I read it, stuck it in my purse and forgot about it.

Now as I sat there looking at the warlock below, I had a desire to give it to *him*. I took it out of my purse and told Irlene, "I'll be back in a few minutes," got up, went up the stairs and into the wide hallway where I retraced my steps to the stairs we had just come up, and hurried down them to the main floor. Once there I made my way to the front, where a small group of ministers or Christian leaders were standing around Eric Pryor, talking with him. The floor level was quite full and the balconies were filling as people poured into them.

Praying in tongues under my breath, I quietly stood about four feet from him on his left, waiting for a chance to speak to him. The men were more or less in a half circle facing him. In a 1991 article in Charisma magazine, writer Steven Lawson described events surrounding Halloween night (the night we missed!), 1990:

> *"Pryor arrived at the civic auditorium in full Wicca priest garb, complete with a huge pentagram around his neck, a ring in his nose, and dressed in black clothes from head to toe. Bernal, having no idea that Pryor was carrying the hidden pistol, escorted him to the front row, close enough to see the whites of Larry Lea's eyes…"*

He was dressed the same Thursday night, though I don't remember a nose ring. What I especially noticed was that he was wearing black leather gloves indoors, as if to ensure no one could touch him. He was very thin, gaunt even, with bleached brassy–blond hair, and a long, angular face. His posture was ramrod straight; he held himself stiffly, to me, it seemed he was on guard. Standing straight and tall in his heeled black boots, he towered over me.

The meeting was going to start soon, and some of the men moved away from him, I presume to go to their seats. He was still standing there, perhaps with Dick Bernal. I reached out and softly tapped the sleeve of his suit jacket.

He turned his head and looked at me. I quickly extended the magazine and said with a smile, "I wanted to give this little magazine to you. I think you might like it—they're all true stories." He accepted it, nodded to me, said "Thank you," and slipped it into his left jacket pocket.

I was filled with joy and thanksgiving as I hurried out an aisle packed with people on both sides, rushed to the stairs and up them as fast as I could (getting slower the higher I went), then back through the hallway to our area, down the balcony steps, and finally dropped beside Irlene, and joyfully whispered to her, "I gave the magazine to him!"

God answers our prayers at unexpected times in unexpected ways sometimes. Though I had no inkling of it, in this first brief contact with Eric Pryor, God was preparing to answer a prayer I had been reminding Him about for two years.

One night about two years before the events in San Francisco, I was at home watching Christian television. Torrey, 5, and Christina, a toddler, were upstairs asleep; Ed was at a meeting. A man was telling his story of how he came to faith in the Lord; I never caught his name.

He said, "I was a Satanist in high school and my friends were the 'Goths.'" ("Goths" is short for Gothics. They're usually young people who seem fascinated with death, wearing black clothes, jewelry with skulls, etc.)

"The Christians ate lunch in a certain area by themselves, and my friends and I ate in another area," he shared. "When I would walk towards where the Christians ate, when they saw me coming, they would all scatter. They would run away and hide; they were afraid of me." As he was talking, the Holy Spirit was stirring in me with compassion.

Then he said, "Don't run when you meet a Satanist. They need Jesus too. Talk to them; tell them about Jesus."

At that point, a strong desire rose up in me. I jumped to my feet, raised my right arm, looked upward towards heaven, and loudly declared, "Lord, I want to meet a Satanist! A high one! And, Lord, if you let it happen, I'll know that You are in charge, and I Won't Be Afraid. I'll know that You allowed it for a reason, and I'll trust You that YOU have a purpose for it—in Jesus' Name!"

The Monday after I prayed it, I was up in the prayer room at church with "Doc" and Irlene. (The three of us prayed together on Monday nights for about six and a half years. We saw many awesome answers to prayer.) Anyway, I shared with them about my prayer to meet a Satanist—a high one!

As soon as I said it, Irlene became alarmed, looked upward and quickly said, "God, that's Donna's prayer—not mine! Lord, that's *her* prayer! I'm not asking for that!" Basically, it was "Leave me out of this, Lord!"

I did *not* have a prayer of agreement on that prayer! Except she agreed *I* could meet a Satanist if I wanted to; she did not want to be included.

Many things happened as a result of that prayer I believe. I reminded the Lord of it regularly—because I meant it. And I wanted it.

***"You did not choose Me, but I chose you and appointed you that you should go and bear fruit, and that your fruit should remain, that whatever you ask the Father in My name He may give you."* (John 15:16). "Thank You, Lord!"**

Chapter 20

Encounter with a Searching Soul

Now there were certain Greeks among those who came to worship at the feast. Then they came near to Phillip, who was from Bethsaida, and asked him, saying, "Sir, we wish to see Jesus."
— John 12:20

The next day, Friday, we attended an afternoon meeting at the Civic Center, then with some ladies we met, walked quite a ways to a restaurant, ate, and returned to the auditorium. Before we went up to the balcony (we sat in the same area as the night before), Irlene said she was going to stop by the restroom and headed toward wide steps leading down to the basement level. "The restrooms are upstairs," I said.

She replied, "There are restrooms down here too." God is so good! This small tidbit of information was important for me to know.

People quietly talked, dozed, or read for the hour and a half until the auditorium started filling up as people began arriving en masse for the closing night of the Breakthrough. At a certain point, we saw Eric Pryor and his fiancée down below in front again, encircled with a group of Christian leaders. One hand was ungloved! I was praising God about this and pointed it out to Irlene and Irene; I knew this was a good sign!

The service was starting; people took their seats, and the music began. By the way, Tim Shepherd's songs and music were stirring and uplifting; they are powerful. During the first or second song, Eric stood up and started down the aisle headed toward the back of the auditorium. A strange feeling came over me. I *knew* he was headed for the restroom in the basement, and I was to go meet him.

There was a power around me. *In the spirit,* I could see tiny flashes of light or energy in the air. Did you ever see when little Tinker Bell would wave her tiny wand and sparkles would follow it? That's the best way I can describe it—except they were just pulsating all around me, not fading or rotating. They were "in place," sparkling and twinkling. I was in an energy field! Looking back, I believe that by the grace of God, the Holy Spirit was anointing me for my meeting with Eric Pryor.

I leaned over to Irlene and said, "I'm going to go meet him!" got up and followed the same route as the night before, except this time I stopped at the opening to the basement and waited there, praying in tongues. My heart was beating fast.

Eric appeared and came up the stairs towards me. I was back three or four feet from the opening; the wall was on my right. Our eyes met, and as he reached the top and came two or three steps forward, I smiled and said, "I met you last night and gave you the little magazine, remember?" He nodded—and then our wonderful talk began. We were all alone with God's presence and protection enveloping us.

I don't remember how it started. I think I told him I was so glad he was there. Looking up into his face, he seemed so fragile to me. I felt such compassion towards him—I know it was God's love for him. We talked, and in the course of our conversation, I asked him what he was looking for; why had he come to the Breakthrough; and how did he become involved with Wicca; although I don't remember in what order we moved from topic to topic.

He told me he was groomed or told from childhood that he had been chosen to be a king. I asked about Wicca and what their beliefs were. He told me they were "white witches," who only used "white magic" to help people. I asked how many were in his group. He told me 35,000. He answered every question I asked, and whether what he told me was true or not, I don't know. All I could do was just listen with my heart. I know my eyes filled with tears several times about some of the things he shared; he seemed so alone and empty to me. I felt such compassion for him. I believe that was part of the anointing from the Holy Spirit.

At one point, he volunteered that he had met with Larry Lea that morning, and Larry had given him a Bible. He took it out of his inside jacket pocket, opened the cover and showed me what Larry had inscribed. I recognized the Bible immediately as one of the slim "military" Bibles Larry had had printed for our troops in the Persian Gulf, I think. I had donated toward their printing myself, and it was such a blessing to see one up close and hold it. I took it in my hands and read what Larry had written.

I do remember gently asking him "Why are you here? What do you want?"

He had replied, "I'm searching for truth."

I think tears were in my eyes; I felt such love for him. Finally, I asked him softly, "Could I pray for you?" He nodded yes.

Gently, I put my opened right hand on his back below his shoulders, in the area of his heart. He was so stiff it was almost like placing my hand on a board. I think my left hand was gripping his arm before the prayer ended.

This may seem strange, but while I was praying for him, in the spirit I "saw" my hand on his back and could also see his heart. He was so cold inside. His heart was encased in ice and as I prayed I could see little "pulses" of heat (love) coming out of my hand and going to his heart. I can see it as I write this. Such a simple little picture the Lord showed me—my hand on his back with little intermittent pulses of love and warmth flowing from my hand, warming him and melting the icy cover around his heart, then flowing into his heart. It was so beautiful to me. The Holy Spirit was using my hand to pour God's love out on him; he needed to know God loved him. The Lord is so kind, loving, and forgiving. His love melts icy hearts and heals hurt ones.

I prayed earnestly, but not loudly; clearly but not abrasively. In looking back, it almost seems God put us in a bubble of some sort for those minutes, on a different plane. One that was quiet, timeless; even the praise music with its powerful under beat of drums and the powerful singing of 6,000 saints inside the auditorium, that had sounded so loud at first, had ceased or was blocked from my hearing, and I believe, from Eric's too. Everything seemed quiet around us.

I remember the prayer, not every word, of course, but I believe the Holy Spirit led me and somehow kept it in my memory. It was very simple. If I had known I was going to be praying with Eric at a certain time and had had several days to think about it and write down what I wanted to pray, I could not have matched it or done half as well.

"Heavenly Father, I praise You. And I thank You for this man who has come here seeking truth. Abba Daddy, JESUS said 'If a son asks for bread, will his father give him a stone? If he asks for a fish, will he give him a serpent?' Holy Father, Jesus is the True Bread that came down from heaven. This man is searching for truth, and I ask that You reveal the Truth to him—that Jesus is Your Son, who died for him, and that everyone who believes on Him shall receive eternal life. Abba Daddy, I ask that he be in heaven someday! Thank You, Heavenly Father. I ask this in Jesus' Holy Name. Amen." As soon as I said "Amen" I heard,

"Amen." "Amen." "Thank You, Lord!" Praise the Lord!" "Yes, Lord." "Amen." There was a chorus of voices in agreement!

Startled, I looked up in surprise and saw men, maybe eight, maybe ten, some with their heads still bowed, standing shoulder to shoulder facing us in a half circle, six to eight feet distance from us. Starting from the opening at the top of the stairs (but not across the opening), they circled us to a point on the wall about eight feet over from where I was standing with Eric. As I glanced around at them in amazement, for I had not known they were there or when they came, the Lord opened my eyes, and I saw in the spirit that angels completed the circle around us. Where the last man stood with his shoulder touching the wall, an angel stood next to him, partially *in* the wall with other angels continuing the circle beyond the wall, across the opening behind Eric, to the man next to the opening. The men and angels had been a shield around us, protecting us from interruption and interference. Later, as I was praying and thanking God for sending His angels to guard us, He showed me the men were encircled by angels too.

I don't know how much of our conversation various ones of them heard, but however much it was, they guarded us while we talked. I will ever be thankful to God for those caring, careful men, who stood silent watch over the woman and the warlock as Jesus poured His love into an empty, searching soul.

I looked up at Eric with love and said, "You want to know truth; God knows your heart. He's going to guide you. He loves you. And I want to see you in heaven someday!"

He was looking down at me as I moved to go, but something made me step back to him, look up at him, and smile. "My name is Donna," I told him. Other people were starting to crowd around him, wanting his attention. I turned and left. We never saw each other again.

"A new commandment I give to you, that you love one another; as I have loved you, that you also love one another. By this all will know that you are My disciples, if you have love one for another." (John 13:14–15).

Chapter 21

The Master's Plan

Why do the nations rage, and the people plot a vain thing? The kings of the earth set themselves, and the rulers take counsel together against the Lord and against His Anointed. He who sits in the heavens shall laugh; The Lord shall hold them in derision.

— Psalms 2:1-2, 4

God so easily views time and events past, present, and future. He created time for mankind, actually, for all of earth's wonderful creatures—animals, fish, even plants; we all live in time. All of earth's processes require time, from baking a cake to plants growing, for life from conception to birth to death.

One time, I was thinking to God about time and eternity, and He showed me a picture to help me understand it. I "saw" a silver cylinder in black space, lying on its side. The cylinder had a beginning and an end—it represented time; time was contained in the cylinder. The limitless space around it represented eternity. God dwells in eternity, or perhaps, eternity dwells in Him.

Now, I want to show you how God will use even things we might view as terrible mistakes or errors in judgment on our part or someone else's, but *He will use those very things to bring about His purpose!*

God knows the end from the beginning, so when the ministers announced they were going to march through Castro District with an estimated 5,000 Christians on Halloween night, and there was such an outcry of rage and indignation from its inhabitants, God had a plan. In hind sight, we can see God's plan unfolding in beautiful sequence as His people prayed.

If that bold announcement, which was later retracted, hadn't been made, I doubt if much notice would have been taken of Christians having their prayer meeting at the Civic Center Auditorium while many San Franciscans celebrated the "Hooker's Ball" in the Castro District. In the 1991 Charisma magazine article, Steven Lawson wrote:

> *"Throughout San Francisco, you'll find psychedelic shops, New Age bookstores ... It's the home of the Church of Satan, the base of operations for homosexual activist group Queer Nation and host of the annual national Hooker's Ball. Each year, a gala Halloween night party draws half a million people to the Castro District, according to some estimates, where many dress in drag and others flaunt sexual promiscuity."*

Of course, the announcement of the march is what drew attention to the Prayer Breakthrough and motivated Eric, in turn, to announce a public cursing, which as stated drew national media attention. And then Eric arranged to be on the local talk show when Pastor Bernal was going to be there, and afterwards, the two of them went to lunch. It was a year later I learned more details through the Charisma article:

> *"While Bernal and Pryor dined, the spiritual warfare was intensifying back at Jubilee Christian Center. Bernal's wife, Carla, was praying for Pryor, believing God would transform his life. That prayer was interrupted by a phone call from C. Peter Wagner. Wagner didn't know about the message or about Pryor's meeting with Bernal. He didn't even know who Pryor was. But Wagner said he believed one of Satan's generals would be won over during the Prayer Breakthrough."*

Well, for quite awhile I didn't associate meeting Eric with my prayer to "meet a Satanist—a high one!" because he was the Wiccan high priest of New Earth Temple in San Francisco, and from what he had told me about Wicca, I didn't think he was a Satanist! (I was naïve about certain matters in 1990 and probably still am.) However, in the 1991 Charisma article, Steven Lawson quoted Eric as saying:

> *"I wasn't about to let anybody else have spiritual control in this city," said Pryor, who openly was a Wicca witch, but secretly was involved in the occult. "I was known somewhat as a general, and I was going to guard my territory."*

So Eric was the real deal; God really did answer my prayer just as I had asked. The Lord is so kind. Even when we don't understand what we're asking for sometimes, if the Lord puts it in our heart, it's because he has a plan to bring it to pass, and a *purpose* for it. But I didn't know any of this that night. Later through the Christian grapevine, sometime after our return home, I heard that Eric Pryor had received the Lord!

Carla Bernal was the Lord's midwife in Eric's new birth and her husband, Dr. Dick Bernal, his spiritual father. They remind me of what Paul wrote to the believers in Corinth, *"For though you might have ten thousand instructors in Christ, yet you do not have many fathers; for in Christ Jesus I have begotten you through the gospel."* (1 Corinthians 4:15).

Steven Lawson also reported in the 1991 article, *"all the top brass from New Earth have now accepted Christ and denounced their former practices."* Hallelujah! So you see, God used the announcement, which many might have thought was a mistake or tactical blunder, to bring precious souls out of darkness into the kingdom of light! And He gave me a once-in-a-lifetime meeting with a very special person that I have prayed for through the years. So, dear Reader, proceed as you are led by the Lord, and trust God for the results.

"I will go before you and make the crooked places straight; I will break in pieces the gates of bronze and cut the bars of iron. I will give you the treasures of darkness and hidden riches of secret places, that you may know that I, the Lord, Who calls you by name, Am the God of Israel." **(Isaiah 45:2–3). How awesome You are, Heavenly Father, the God of Israel!**

CHAPTER 22

JOURNEY'S END

But if the Spirit of Him who raised Jesus from the dead dwells in you, He who raised Christ from the dead will also give life to your mortal bodies through His Spirit who dwells in you.

— **Romans 8:11**

In preparing to write about meeting Eric, I decided to contact him, nearly twenty-five years after we met. To my sorrow, I learned that Eric's earthly journey had ended. He was killed in June of 2009, struck by a truck as he was crossing the street. He was only 49.

I read his obituary, and an article in Charisma Magazine titled, "Wiccan-Turned-Bible-Teacher Eric Pryor Dies" written by Adrienne Gaines, published June 16, 2009. Pastor Dick Bernal was quoted as follows:

> *"Eric's passion was to convert the Wiccan people and people that are spiritual but going down the wrong path," said Bernal, who remained Pryor's*

> *friend and mentor. "He used to say, 'Pastor Dick, I need to get my friends out of darkness.' That was his passion—not really preaching to the choir or preaching to saved people. His passion was to…persuade people who were following false religions, even demonic, satanic beliefs. That was his desire."*

Jesus said, *"Do not lay up for yourselves treasure on earth where moth and rust destroy and thieves break in and steal; but lay up for yourselves treasures in heaven, where neither moth nor rust destroy and where thieves do not break in and steal. For where your treasure is, there your heart will be also."* (Matthew 6:19–21). People are earth's greatest treasure. Eric loved people; under the Lord, they were his treasure.

I thank God for letting me meet Eric. Our time together was brief, but divinely appointed. I rejoice that he received the Lord and served Him faithfully to the end of his days. At every ending is a new beginning; I will see Eric in heaven some day.

"Martha said to Him, 'I know that he will rise again in the resurrection at the last day.' Jesus said to her, "I am the resurrection and the life. He who believes in Me, though he may die, he shall live. And whoever lives and believes in Me shall never die. Do you believe this?" She said to Him, 'Yes, Lord, I believe that You are the Christ, the Son of God, who is to come into the world.'" **(John 11: 24–27). I believe this also.**

Chapter 23

Homeward Bound

And the hand of our God was upon us, and He delivered us from the hand of the enemy and from ambush along the road.
— Ezra 8:1b

Thursday night in the throng at the Breakthrough, Irlene and I had bumped into Jim, a brother from our own home church in Walnut. We hadn't known the other was there. We told him about my car and that we were using a rental. He said that after the Breakthrough, he would follow us to Bakersfield; we could turn in the car, and he would give us a ride home. So through Jim, the Lord graciously provided a ride from Bakersfield for us.

God used Larry Lea to plant a seed of faith in my spirit about a significant, even startling, truth through something he taught about at the Prayer Breakthrough, and it has proven true in my life. It is based on the story of David, who returned to Ziklag with his 600 men to discover the town had been attacked while they were away. The whole account is in I Samuel 30.

"Now it happened, when David and his men came to Ziklag, on the third day, that the Amalekites had invaded the South and Ziklag, attacked Ziklag and burned it with fire, and had taken captive the women and those who were there, from small to great; they did not kill anyone, but carried them away and went their way.

"Then David and the people who were with him lifted up their voices and wept, until they had no more power to weep. And David's two wives, Ahinoam … and Abigail … had been taken captive.

"Then David was greatly distressed, for the people spoke of stoning him, because the soul of all the people was grieved, every man for his sons and his daughters. But David strengthened himself in the Lord." We should do this too in times of distress or need!

"… So David inquired of the Lord, saying, 'Shall I pursue this troop? Shall I overtake them?'

"And He answered him, 'Pursue, for you shall surely overtake them and without fail recover all.'

"So David went, he and the six hundred men who were with him, and came to the Brook Besor, where those stayed who were left behind. But David pursued, he and four hundred men,

for two hundred stayed behind, who were so weary that they could not cross the Brook Besor.

"Then they found an Egyptian in the field, and brought him to David; and they gave him bread and he ate, and they let him drink water. And they gave him a piece of a cake of figs and two clusters of raisins. So when he had eaten, his strength came back to him, for he had eaten no bread nor drunk any water for three days and three nights."

Note: The Jewish people are a very generous people—and merciful, even to their captives. It turned out this young man's master had left him behind to die because he was sick. His master was an Amalekite, one of the troop that had attacked and burned Ziklag, as well as other cities and villages of Judah, a southern part of Israel.

"And David said to him, 'Can you bring me down to this troop?'

"And he said, 'Swear to me by God that you will neither kill me nor deliver me into the hands of my master, and I will take you down to this troop.' So when he had brought him down, there they were, spread out over all the land, eating and drinking and dancing, because of all the great spoil which they had taken from the land of the Philistines and from the land of Judah.

"And David attacked them from twilight until the evening of the next day. Not a man of them

> *escaped, except four hundred young men who rode on camels and fled. So David recovered all the Amalekites had carried away, and David rescued his two wives." (1 Samuel 30:1-18)*

I believe David's two wives had been comforting the other captives, women, and children, and encouraging them not to give up—to take heart, because his wives *knew* David would come after them and rescue them. David was a mighty warrior, a great leader, but more than that, they knew David loved God with all his heart, and *God loved him and was with him*! Hallelujah! Oh, how wonderful it is to be in the loving care of our great God!

"He who dwells in the secret place of the Most High shall abide under the shadow of the Almighty. I will say of the Lord, 'He is my refuge and my fortress; my God, in Him I will trust.'" (Psalms 91:1-2).

"So David recovered all the Amalekites had carried away, and David rescued his two wives." But that wasn't all! *"And nothing of theirs was lacking, either small or great, sons or daughters, spoil or anything which they had taken from them; David recovered all. Then David took all the flocks and herds which they had driven before those other livestock, and said, 'This is David's spoil.'" (1 Samuel 30:19–20)*

The amount of livestock and goods they won must have been tremendous because David sent presents from it to at least 15 cities, to the elders of Judah, and to his friends, saying, "Here is a present for you from the spoil of the enemies of the Lord."

Larry's point was *what the enemy has stolen from us, we can recover* as our Heavenly Father told David, *"Pursue, for you shall surely overtake them and without fail* ***recover all.****"* (1 Samuel 30:8b).

I believe he connected this to Proverbs 6:31, speaking of a thief. *"Yet when he is found, he must restore sevenfold."* A simplified rendering is, "When the thief is discovered, he must repay seven times." These two scriptures, one on recovering and the other on restitution, or *compensation,* have been connected in my mind for 25 years. And God has used it mightily!

The Breakthrough ended Friday night. As Irlene, Irene, and I were driving to meet Jim Saturday morning, I was in the backseat meditating on the word of God, thinking about my car engine blowing up and what Larry had said about recovering it all. A holy indignation began to rise up in me—I had taken my car to a shop the previous Saturday and paid $149 for a tune up, lube job, and two new tires for the trip. So I felt like I had done due diligence preparing my car, and now it had been stolen from me. Then there was the cost of renting a car for four days; even though Irlene's insurance covered that. And we had missed the first night of the Breakthrough, which I felt was stolen from me. (Maybe I got it back seven times over by meeting Eric and writing about it now to encourage *you* to pursue what has been stolen from you.) And I still didn't know how much it was going to cost to repair my car.

Well, the more I thought about it, the more I felt a holy determination; the devil had stolen from me, and I wanted it back-—seven times over! So I told Irlene and Irene I was going to ask God that everything that had been stolen from me would be repaid *seven times over.* They said they would agree with me for that, so with them agreeing, I prayed out loud, and it was pretty loud!

After the prayer, I wrote down on a piece of paper that the three of us had agreed in prayer in JESUS' name, that "everything that had been stolen from me, the devil MUST pay back—seven times over, based on the word of God that 'When the thief is discovered he must repay seven times.'" I put the date on the paper, signed it, and passed it to the front seat for both of them to sign, which they did. Hallelujah! So I had it in writing that the devil owed me seven times more than what all this was going to cost—based on the word of God. Praise God!

I will tell you how God worked it out, and the devil had to repay everything he took from me. He had to repay or release from the world's system seven times more than the costs of everything that was stolen. He has to obey God, and *God honors His Word above His Name!* (Psalms 138:2).

One other thing happened on the way back home that is worth mentioning, in case you ever find yourself in a similar situation.

When we met up with Jim to caravan to Bakersfield, Irene remained with Irlene and I rode with Jim to keep him company. Late that afternoon, the four of us stopped for dinner together at a nice restaurant by the freeway, maybe 90 miles out from Bakersfield. I don't remember if Jim didn't fill the gas tank then, because he thought there might be a better price closer to Bakersfield; or if he just forgot about it until we were some miles down the freeway and there was nothing available. He said several times, "I should have gotten gas back there where we ate. It's almost on empty!"

At a certain place, he turned off the freeway onto a road to the right thinking it would lead to a small town where he could get gas. But very shortly, we were out in farm country on a two-lane road with both fenced and unfenced fields on both sides of us. Sometimes we could see miles ahead and around us with nothing in sight, except an occasional farm house a long way off. We had to go long distances sometimes until we'd come to a lonely stop sign with another two-lane road crossing in front of us, but with no road sign to let us know where we were. The sun was low in the sky by now.

Jim was getting really worried—we were practically out of gas; we were off the freeway in farm country with no knowledge of exactly where we were. We had no phone available and no where to find one.

"Jim, let's pray in tongues," I said and began to do so.

He did for a moment, but concern about our situation was overtaking him. "We're going to run out! It's *below* empty!"

Authority (or perhaps it was faith) rose up in me, and I said, "No, we're not! Pray in tongues!" and then I prayed loudly in English.

"Father, in Jesus name, we ask that You *extend* the gas in this tank—that it be multiplied just as Jesus broke the bread and fish and fed five thousand men, and women and children! We pray that there be enough gas in this car to get us to a gas station, where we can fill it up. And we also ask that You lead us to a gas station, Abba Daddy. We don't know where we are, but You do. Please put angels around us to help us! Thank you, Father! In Jesus' name we pray!"

Jim agreed with a fervent, "Amen!"

"Pray in tongues!" I said again and did so myself—urgently. Somehow, I think both of us felt the crisis point was approaching. Then came a moment when the power ceased, the engine was silent, and the car slowed.

Jim said, "We're out!" I, too, felt the gas was gone, and God would have to help us by having the car run supernaturally. I was praying earnestly and loudly in tongues so was Jim!

The car abruptly slowed and coasted a few seconds. All of a sudden, it picked up speed! The engine *restarted*, and we could feel power again! It is my belief it switched from gas to Faith in that moment. Hallelujah!

Jim must have felt the same thing because he said, "It ran out! I felt the moment it ran out, then it started again!" He had a look of wonderment on his face and began to thank God, which I was already doing. After a few more minutes, he let out a sigh of relief and relaxed. With joy and praise, we continued to thank our Father in heaven!

We drove at least 45 minutes more as the sky darkened, finally coming to a road with a sign indicating the freeway was to the left 18 or 19 miles! We gladly took the road and finally saw a light far ahead. When we got close, we saw it was a gas station. We had veered away from the freeway and had to go 18 miles or so to reach a little gas station on the other side of the freeway. We pulled in, filled the tank, and then found out we were nearly 40 miles on the *other* side of Bakersfield. Bakersfield was about 40 miles *behind* us!

Jim was able to call Irlene at the car rental place, tell her what had happened and that we would drive *back* to Bakersfield to get them! But in spite of this, we were praising the Lord and rejoicing as we drove back. There had been that definite moment when we both felt the gas was gone and the car started running supernaturally as God answered our *fervent* prayers.

"The effective, fervent prayer of a righteous man avails much!" (James 5:16b). "Thank You, Jesus!"

Jim never forgot it either. Sometime later, he started going to a smaller church closer to his home. Ed and I, with Torrey and Christina, visited there once to hear a certain speaker who was holding a meeting there; this was 4 or 5 years after the Prayer Breakthrough. We didn't know that was Jim's new church; we hadn't seen him for several years.

When Jim saw us and after we had joyfully greeted each other, he said, "Donna, I'll never forget that time we ran out of gas coming back from San Francisco. It was amazing! I knew exactly when the gas was all gone, and the car just kept going!"

You know, dear Reader, we are not the first people this has happened to—having a car run on an empty tank when there is a great need. God loves us. Sometimes there is no place to turn, except to God!

"They wandered in the wilderness in a desolate way; they found no city to dwell in … Then they cried out to the Lord in their trouble, and He delivered them out of their distresses. And He led them forth by the right way, that they might go to a city for habitation. Oh, that men would give thanks to the Lord for His goodness, and for His wonderful works to the children of men." **(Psalms 107:4–8)! Amen, and "Thank You, Abba Daddy!"**

Chapter 24

The Seed Is In the Soil

Therefore be patient, brethren, until the coming of the Lord. See how the farmer waits for the precious fruit of the earth, waiting patiently for it, until it receives the early and latter rain.
— James 5:7

Waiting for a prayer to be answered or for a promise of God to be fulfilled requires patience. As I wrote earlier, earth's processes take time. Well, heaven's promises and processes require time too, and patience. Though sometimes prayers are answered quickly in breathtaking and spectacular ways, most prayers are answered over a period of time. Little by little, changes come.

My prayer of conviction that everything stolen from me on the trip, the devil *must* restore seven times over took 20 months to fulfill, but it happened, and this is how.

I didn't know how much the devil owed me because I didn't know how much was stolen. It was three weeks before Ed and a friend were able to go to Bakersfield to tow back my car. He arranged with a brother at church, a mechanic who owned a garage, to keep my car there and work on it with his help, paying him a certain sum. Ed located a rebuilt engine for my car at a cost of $895, had to remove the ruined engine, install the other one, add new parts such as hoses, belts, etc. That took several more weeks.

I figured out as best I could what the losses were: the $149 I had paid for the tune up and new tires before our trip (yes, the car still had the tires, but I felt the devil owed me the full amount on general principles); the towing charge to Bakersfield and the car rental for four days (though technically, I hadn't paid for either of those, I still figured the devil owed it back seven times); Ed's roundtrip up there to get my car; the *inconvenience* of being without my own car for weeks; the rebuilt engine, miscellaneous expenses, *and* as I told the Lord, "Ed's labor is worth something!" By my calculations, it was between $2,500 and $3,000. Multiplied seven times, it rounded up to $18,000 to $21,000.

Anyway, after I had arrived at an amount, one morning in my prayer closet (which for 14 years in the townhouse was the laundry room where I prayed and read the word on my knees), I laid out all the facts before the Lord, along with my written-out prayer of agreement which Jim, as well as Irlene and Irene, had also signed. And most importantly and pertinently, the Word of God, which said "When the thief is discovered, he must repay seven times!"

After going over all the facts with Abba Daddy, our Heavenly Father, I said, "God, I don't know exactly how much it is, but You know how much it is *to the penny*, so I ask that the devil be forced to pay me back seven times what was stolen from me—that he must *release it to me* from the world's system!"

Then, in the presence of Heavenly Father, the Righteous Judge of the earth, I said to the devil, trusting that God would make him hear my "lawsuit" or righteous claim, "Satan, according to the Word of God in Proverbs 6:31, 'When the thief is discovered, he must repay seven times,' I tell you in the Name of the Lord JESUS, that you have to restore to me *seven times* what was stolen from me! It's between $18,000 and $21,000. I don't know exactly how much it is, but GOD DOES to the penny, and He will tell you what it is, and you have to repay it to me from the world's system—in Jesus' mighty Name!"

Then I held out my left hand and struck the palm twice with my right hand, while I strongly said, "Right here, Satan! Right here, in the palm of my hand! I expect a Check for whatever amount the Lord tells you—in Jesus' name! Thank You, Abba Daddy, in Jesus' name!"

Dear Reader, I never doubted or backed off from that prayer *one second* in the next twenty months, the amount of time it took to receive the answer to my prayer. I *knew* the Lord had heard me and it *would* be answered. *"Now this is the confidence that we have in Him, that if we ask anything according to His will, He hears us. And if we know that He hears us, whatever we ask, we know that we have the petitions that we have asked of Him"* (1John 5:14–15). The seed was in the soil…and a properly cultivated and watered seed will grow and produce fruit.

Every few months, I would remind the Lord *and the devil* about it. I would Thank the Lord that He was answering my prayer; then I would hold out my left hand, pat the palm and say to the devil, "Satan, right here! Right in my hand! I expect a check for the amount the Lord told you to give me!"

Well, to make a long story short, one year later *to the day* after my car engine blew up, Irlene and I drove to San Francisco again, to attend a prayer gathering at Candlestick Park with Larry Lea. We were in a rental car this time, and two other ladies went with us. I was sitting in the back seat behind Irlene who was driving. This is the accident mentioned in chapter 11, "Healing Is the Children's Bread." It was pouring down rain as we inched along on the backed-up freeway exit to the park, and we were rear ended by a car driven by an older gentleman. It was quite a jolt, but no dents or scraped paint except a small two-inch mark on the back bumper. This concerned, honest older gentleman gave me his name and insurance information in drenching rain and later reported it to his insurance company. I reported it too, after we returned home.

After we were back and Irlene was going to turn in the car, she asked me if she should tell the agency about the accident. I said, "Yes! We have to tell them; God can't bless us if we don't tell them."

When she told the man about the other car hitting us, he walked out to the lot, looked at the little mark and said, "It's all right. These are new bumpers that move, so the car is fine. There's no damage." Praise the Lord! We have to keep short accounts with the Lord.

I was the secretary of a small security company at the time and did a lot of typing, record keeping, and answering the phone, so I was seated quite a bit. By the second or third day back at work, my back began to hurt and pains began to shoot down my left leg. The pain became more intense over the next few days, so I called the older gentleman's insurance company and was told to go to a doctor and have it checked.

The doctor said, "The worst thing you could do is be sitting all day!" He put me on temporary disability and ordered treatments for my back, neck and shoulders. I was on medical leave for three months and continued to receive treatments for several months, even after I was cleared to return to work. My back, neck, right shoulder, and arm had been injured.

When my condition stabilized and costs (treatments, lost wages, mileage for doctor appointments, etc.) had been submitted, Ed and I met with the insurance representative. She carefully went over all the reports and paperwork, added *compensation* for pain and suffering then offered me a settlement, which I accepted. A check for $20,000 was *placed in my hand* that day in June, 1992. "Thank You, Jesus!"

Remember I had told the Lord it was between $18,000 and $21,000? That I didn't know exactly how much, but HE did, to the penny? Well, it turned out the doctor's office hadn't submitted its last bill to the insurance company before we settled, so they sent it to me. I received a bill for $564, I think, and some cents. I paid it out of the settlement, so the final total of what the devil (thief) had to repay, was $19,435 and some *pennies*! Praise the Lord! God is faithful and His word is true. Then in November of that year, the Lord *healed* my back, neck, arm and shoulder at the Benny Hinn Crusade in Long Beach, CA (Chapter 11)! "Thank You, Jesus!"

If you are a believer, I believe *you* too can recover the value of things that have been stolen from you, if you present a "legal claim" for it to the Lord *based on the word of God*—and the devil has to repay, sometimes seven times more than what was stolen. "Thank You, Jesus!"

"For whatever is born of God overcomes the world. And this is the victory that overcomes the world—our faith. Who is he who overcomes the world, but he who believes that Jesus is the Son of God?" **(1 John 5:4–5) Amen!**

CHAPTER 25

IN ELEVEN YEARS I HAVEN'T RECEIVED ONE CENT OF CHILD SUPPORT!

People do not despise a thief if he steals because he is starving, yet when he is found, he must restore seven times.

— Proverbs 6: 30–31a

"Donna, cousin Sharon said to tell you that everything you two prayed about at the family reunion has happened. She said, 'God has answered every one of those prayers.'" Fast forward to 2004; we were living in San Antonio now, and I was talking to my sister, Rebecca, in Alaska on the phone one day when she relayed this message to me.

My response was rapid and joyful, "Praise the Lord, Rebecca! Hallelujah!" I remembered very well the day Sharon and I had prayed together.

At a family reunion in Oregon in 1998, Sharon had invited me to her sister's house just up the road from where many family members were camping in tents and trailers. Once there, she fixed us iced tea, and since the house appeared empty, began to share some things. That day she told me, "In eleven years, I haven't received one cent of child support!" (Sharon's about ten years younger than me.)

She shared with me how difficult things had been after Pete (*not her former husband's real name*) had left her and their three small children after becoming involved with a woman where he worked and with whom he had started smoking marijuana. He had divorced Sharon, and he and the woman had married.

Sharon had been given custody of the children and was awarded child support, which she received regularly for 6 years; but eventually the drug use had cost Pete and his new wife their jobs, and the child support payments stopped coming.

Sharon had forgiven them long ago and asked me to pray for Pete and his wife because she had serious health problems and was very sick. They were also receiving food stamps because Pete's earnings were minimal.

After listening for awhile, I said, "Sharon, as a believer, a child of God which you are, you have a right to get that child support back seven times over." I then gave her a summary of the trip to San Francisco, my car engine being ruined and how I had presented a "claim" or request to God for all those related costs to be repaid to me out of the world's system *by the devil*—seven times over! I quoted the scripture in Proverbs 6:30–31 about the thief, who, when discovered *must* repay seven times, and how I did get it back seven times over!

"Sharon, that money was stolen from you by the devil. You were awarded that child support legally by the judge, and it is lawfully owed to you. The devil stole it through sin when he enslaved Pete and his wife with the drugs, which caused them to lose their jobs and everything else that's happened to them. Do you want to ask the Lord for all that back child support—seven times over?"

I could tell this was a new concept for her, one "out of the blue" so to speak (I call it the "heavenly blue"). We talked a little more; I was also quietly praying in tongues, when I could do so unobtrusively. Then a thought came to me:

"Sharon, there's another place in the Old Testament where it says if someone steals a sheep, he has to give back four sheep for the one he stole. Would you be more comfortable with a four-times return instead of seven?"

You know, dear Reader, you can start where your faith is. Here is an example: In his inspiring book, *The Fourth Dimension*, Dr. David Yonggi Cho tells how as a young minister he learned a great truth (he was called Paul Yonggi Cho when the book was first published in 1979).

After spending hours in Bible study and prayer each week, when he got up to preach, he would "see" pictures and scenes. He wrote "…it was as if I were watching television. On my mind's screen, I could see growths disappear, tuberculosis healed, cripples leaning heavily on crutches suddenly throw them aside and walk."

Since he was untaught about these "pictures" (visions), he concluded they were from the devil; that "a spirit of hindrance" was trying to confuse him and make him forget his sermon! He would dismiss the pictures and try to gather his thoughts to preach the sermon, and later, during his prayer times, he would command a spirit of hindrance to leave him, but the more he commanded a hindering spirit to leave, the more pictures he "saw." He became desperate for them to stop. They were coming continually; so in desperation, he made it a subject of prayer and fasting, waiting on the Lord.

Well, one day in his spirit, he heard, "Son, that is not a hindrance of Satan. That is the *visual desire* of the Holy Spirit. It is the word of wisdom and of knowledge. God wants to heal these people, but God can't heal them before you speak."

He was stunned by this but finally decided to speak out the healings. He started by declaring the simplest of what he was seeing: a person being healed of a headache. And the person was instantly healed. Gradually he began to speak out the other "visual desires of the Holy Spirit" that he saw, and people came out of wheelchairs, received their sight, and were healed of ailments and conditions too numerous to mention here.

My point here is that I felt through the Lord, a seven-times more return was more than Sharon could believe for right then; after all, she had never heard of anything like this before! BUT she could be in agreement for a four-times more return on eleven years of unpaid, "stolen" child support payments. She said, "Yes" for the four-times more restoration.

I asked, "How much were the monthly payments?"

She told me and we calculated the annual amount of twelve payments, multiplied that *eleven* times for the total amount stolen from her by the devil over the last eleven years. Adjusted slightly that came out to $37,000; then we multiplied that by four for the "four-times more" restoration. It came out to $148,000, praise the Lord! That is a very nice sum, a windfall for anyone.

I said, "Sharon, let's write this down and sign it—that we have *agreed* according to the word of God for a full recovery of the amount stolen and a four-times more restoration!

She got me a sheet of paper and a pen, and I wrote out an agreement similar to this and we signed it.

"On this day of June 17, 1998, Donna Hamilton and Sharon (name withheld), agree in prayer, based on the Word of God, that the child support payments that have been stolen from her by the devil for the last eleven years, MUST be repaid to her four-times Over the stolen amount! The monthly payments of $280 amount to $3,360 per year; multiplied by eleven years comes to $37,000, which multiplied four times is $148,000. We Agree on this according to the Word of God. We present this prayer request in JESUS' Name! "Thank You, Father!" We both signed it *under* Jesus' name because we were presenting our petition/lawsuit/claim in HIS name!

Well, after Rebecca gave me Sharon's message that "Everything we prayed about has happened—God has answered every one of those prayers," I called her. This is what she told me:

"Donna, the week after you prayed, Pete got a job that paid him *two and a half times* what he had been making! He paid every bit of the back child support payments. I used that money for a down payment on a two-bedroom house for my children and me. When Mom got sick (*Aunt Betty, her Mom, was fighting cancer),* I sold the house, and that's when I got back four times more! With that I was able to get a three-bedroom house so Mom could live with us." Praise the Lord! What a blessing that was because Sharon took care of her Mom until she went to heaven. Sharon is still in that house today.

Isn't that an awesome testimony! Only God could work out something like that. It is amazing, but GOD is an awesome God, and He does amazing things. "Oh, the depths of the riches, both of the wisdom and knowledge of God! How unsearchable are His *judgments* and His ways past finding out!" (Romans 11:33). Hallelujah!

She made a profit of $148,000 on the sale of the little two-bedroom house. Home prices in California were rising dramatically in those years. I am sure the Lord led her to the exact house to buy and opened the door for her to purchase it and, of course, later brought the buyers. God is so faithful to keep His promises.

Now, dear Reader, what are *you* going to do about things that have been stolen from *you* through the years? By the way, I once heard someone in ministry say "the Lord told her to give her fur coat to someone, but she didn't do it. Six weeks later their travel bus was broken into, and the only thing taken was the fur coat!" Was it "unlawfully stolen" or in this case, did disobedience give Satan "legal" access to it? I do not know. Please "wait upon the Lord" about everything taken from you. Do as David did after he and his men returned to Ziklag and found the city burned and everything stolen:

"So David inquired of the Lord, saying, 'Shall I pursue this troop? Shall I overtake them?'

"And He answered him, 'Pursue, for you shall surely overtake them and without fail recover all.'" (1Samuel 30: 8).

Personally, I would not go after everything in a lump sum. For instance, if a house you owned burned down through no fault of your own, and you did not have Personal Property insurance, and therefore, had a loss of personal belongings. Banks require homeowners insurance on houses, so replacement costs are usually covered; however, there would be a lot of *sorrow* and *inconvenience* through this! I asked for, and received, *compensation* for the inconvenience of being without my car for six weeks. Then, say, one of your cars was stolen at another time; I would not combine those two thefts or losses together; I would figure out the "scriptural" restoration amount for each item, and write those up as two separate "claims," then present them to the Lord in prayer. God is so wise and fair. He is the Righteous Judge of the earth!

"He shall judge the world in righteousness, and He shall administer ***judgment*** *for the peoples in righteousness."* (Psalms 9: 8). "Thank You, Holy Father!"

Here are several scriptures that might guide you in what you can/should ask for. Please ask precious Holy Spirit to lead you in this.

"If a man steals an ox or a sheep, and slaughters it or sells it, he should restore five oxen for an ox and four sheep for a sheep…If the theft is certainly found alive in his hand, whether it is an ox or donkey or sheep, he shall restore double." (Exodus 22: 1,4). So even if the item were recovered, the owner would still get back "double for his trouble" (my words, not scripture's). The thief would have to repay double. There are additional scriptures in Exodus 22 relating to stolen or ruined property you might consider.

And, of course, there is the one I felt impressed to present to Abba Daddy regarding my car engine being ruined and the costs and losses related to that—including compensation for the *inconvenience* of being without my car for six weeks or so and having to adjust my and the kids' schedules, in order to use Ed's car for grocery shopping, errands, etc.. The simplified version is *"When the thief is discovered, he must repay seven times."* (Proverbs 6: 30-31).

I am not Jewish, nor am I a Hebrew scholar. My understanding of these ordinances is simplistic and uninstructed, probably laughable to a Rabbi or Hebrew scholar. Nevertheless, God honored my scripture–based, faith-filled request that Satan repay to me from the world's system, *seven times* the theft and losses related to my car engine blowing up. And six years later, He honored by answering, the prayer of agreement with my cousin that her unpaid child support payments (eleven years worth!) be restored four times over. This happened through a process that unfolded over six years, following our prayer.

Just receiving the back payments alone was a wonderful praise report, but then to have them multiplied and restored *four times over* is amazing, except that it was based on the word of God and demonstrates the truth, power and authority of His word.

So now, dear Reader, I leave these true stories in your hands. If I have been able to fan your faith in God, our wonderful heavenly Father, that He loves you and all of heaven is pulling for you, cheering you on and desiring to see you move forward and step out in faith to do mighty things for God, in JESUS' name, to help others here on earth, then I rejoice!

May we all walk in our callings and each of us complete our God–appointed assignments. At the Last Supper, the night He was betrayed, *"Jesus spoke these words, lifted up His eyes to heaven and said, 'Father, the hour has come. Glorify Your Son, that Your Son also may glorify You… I have glorified You on the earth. I have finished the work which You have given Me to do…'"* (John 17:1,4). One of the last things He said on the cross was *"It is finished."* (John 19:30). At the end of our lives here on earth, may we say the same.

You are important; your life matters. What you do makes a difference to others, including future generations. Your journey is woven into others, and together God uses us to demonstrate His love and goodness, even his judgments. Thereby, through His grace, we help bring forth the will of God on earth.

"Our Father in heaven, hallowed be Your name. Your kingdom come; Your will be done on earth, as it is in heaven. Give us this day our daily bread. And forgive us our debts as we forgive our debtors. And do not lead us into temptation, but deliver us from the evil one. For Yours is the kingdom and the power and the glory forever. Amen." **(Matthew 6:9b–13). Selah.**

How to Receive Jesus as Lord and Savior

"So I sought for a man among them who would make a wall, and stand in the gap before Me on behalf of the land, that I should not destroy it, but I found no one. Therefore I have poured out My indignation on them; I have consumed them with the fire of My wrath; and I have recompensed their deeds on their own heads," says the Lord God.

—Ezekiel 22:30-31

Jesus, the holy and sinless Son of God, made a wall, and stood in the gap before God for us and all mankind for our salvation, so that God the Father would not destroy us for our sins. Jesus willingly and knowingly came to earth for the specific purpose of offering Himself to take our place and receive the punishment or wages (payment) of our sin so the *righteous* judgment of God and was destroyed received and when you receive Him to be your Lord and Savior and God, the Righteous Judge of the earth, poured out His indignation on HIM instead of us; He consumed HIM with the fire of His wrath instead of consuming each of us, and He recompensed our wicked deeds upon HIS HEAD, the Lamb of God, the Great Shepherd of the Sheep, for us.

If you have not asked Jesus to be your Savior, please do so now. Pray this prayer:

A Sinner's Prayer

"Father God, I believe Jesus is Your only begotten Son, and He came to earth, born as a baby. He lived a sinless life, so that death had no claim on Him but He laid down His life for my sake and died on the cross for my sins. Please forgive my sins, and come into my heart now, Lord Jesus. I will serve You and love You forever. I ask the Holy Spirit to come into my heart now. Thank You, Heavenly Father! In Jesus' name, I pray. Amen."

Epilogue: The Lord Is a Warrior

For as many as are led by the Spirit of God, these are sons of God... The Spirit Himself bears witness with our spirit that we are children of God.
— Romans 8: 14,16

Dear Reader, the Lord wants to tell us things; things that will help us in our own lives and families, and He also wants to show us things that will help other people in their lives and in their families in their needs. There are situations God wants changed and problems people have with which He wants to help, but to do that, God needs *prayer* asking Him to help! And prayer requires *pray-ers,* people who pray. Someone, somewhere, needs to pray about the situations God wants changed. Someone, somewhere, needs to pray about the problems people have, with which God wants to help.

God has a solution for every problem; a way through every difficulty, provision for every need. But He has set up the world so that people have to ask Him to help, ask for His solutions—ask Him to intervene. Remember *He gave man dominion over the earth,* and He set up natural laws that operate for everyone: man or woman, saint or sinner, young or old, great or small. For these laws to be suspended or for supernatural events to manifest or for amazing only-God-could-have-done-it things to transpire, prayer must rise from humble, submitted hearts.

The Lord wants to have vessels (persons) through whom He can work, to whom He can show the things He wants to do; even someone to whom He can show the needs of other people. Someone He can trust to *love* them, not judge them for their mistakes, sins, or shortcomings. Will you be a person God can trust with others' hurts and sorrows?

It is written of Jesus, *"He was a man of sorrow, acquainted with grief, and we hid, as it were, our faces from Him."* (Isaiah 53:3). Yes, you might look funny to the world when you are looking at a newscast and suddenly burst into tears because sorrow overcomes you, and deep sobs rise from your innermost being, and you begin to pray (sometimes in tongues) for that person or situation, but God can do a lot through those tears and those prayers. He can help that young mother who lost a child or that young man who was in a terrible accident or correct an injustice.

The Lord wants you to have listening ears to receive so He can reveal things to you. Look at the way He took His disciples aside and told them things to come; also the way He explained parables to them in private. He usually ended with *"He that has ears to hear, let him hear!"* (Mark 7:16 and Matthew 13:43). I believe He longs to do this with every person who has received Him as Savior. But there is a cost, and that cost is spending time with Him on a regular basis, just sitting in His presence, quietly worshipping, perhaps with your open Bible before you and reading the Word of God, sometimes meditating on just a verse or two, sometimes reading several chapters, presenting needs and concerns to God, both yours and others.

If you will do this, you will discover the Lord will also speak to you outside of your prayer closet. You may be driving down a freeway as I was, when He told me that Michael and Michelle didn't want their baby born in November. That was a revelation; something that had never entered my head. Any number of exciting adventures and awesome encounters will begin to happen to you. You will be at the right place at the right time to witness, or be a part of, great events; for God to "bless you and make you be a blessing" to others. He will use your faith along with your knowledge of His word, to solve problems for others, to get answers to prayer for them that they need—sometimes answers that they desperately need.

Just as a matter of reference, for years it was my custom to read while on my knees, ten chapters a day in my Bible: four consecutive chapters (which will take you through the Bible in a year); five Psalms (I had read somewhere that Dr. Billy Graham reads five psalms a day so I decided to do the same); and one chapter of Proverbs which basically took me through the book of Proverbs once a month.

There are 31 chapters in Proverbs, so if you read Chapter One on the first day of the month and Chapter Two on the second, and so forth—and continue this throughout the year, you will read through the Proverbs twelve times a year. If you do this and meditate on them, I believe that over time, wisdom will guide you. That is why King Solomon wrote them!

> *"To give prudence to the simple, To the young man—knowledge and discretion— A wise man will hear and increase learning, And a man of understanding will attain wise counsel, To understand a proverb and an enigma, The words of the wise and their riddles."* (Proverbs 1:4-6)

I have come to believe people are sometimes given prayer assignments just as much as they are given ministry assignments. I'm sure you have heard of people awakened in the night, or during the day while busy with some activity, suddenly receiving a heavy prayer burden about a specific matter.

Let me put it this way; there are times when I have desired something for myself or someone else and perceive it would be according to God's will for certain things to happen, so I pray along those lines, but there have been other times when, not out of my own choosing nor out of any "decision" on my part, mighty prayer burdens have come upon me. I'll share one of them as an example.

In August 1988, Shi'a gunmen hijacked a Kuwait Airways plane with more than 110 people on board and forced it to land in Algiers. In a terrifying siege that lasted 16 grueling days in three or four different mid-eastern cities, two Kuwaitis were brutally killed. The whole saga was covered by international media. The hijackers threatened to blow up the plane, including themselves with all the passengers—if the Kuwait government did not release 17 terrorist prisoners, which it refused to do. They were at an impasse.

The first Monday night a few days after the hijacking, when Doc, Irlene, and I met for our weekly prayer time, I'm not sure we even prayed about it. But as that week progressed, I became very disturbed in my spirit by the news reports—the death threats, harsh demands, and treatment of the hostages that were still held.

The women, children, and elderly were eventually released as the hijackers felt they could obtain their object with using just the men as hostages. I have since learned that hijackers don't like to have "high need" hostages; it's too much trouble and too unpredictable. Plus it diminishes sympathy for the hijackers and their "cause." Before the week was over, I *knew* we were to pray about it the coming Monday night. The burden was so heavy on me.

The following Monday night, five or six new people came up to the prayer room wanting us to pray for them! This was the largest number of first-timers that ever came at one time during the nearly seven years the three of us met to pray. It took a long time to pray for them individually, breaking generational bondages then anointing each one and dedicating him/her to the Lord. God had told Doc several years before, that the first time someone came up to the prayer room, we were to do this. Plus, they each had prayer requests they wanted prayed about. One by one, they left after they were prayed for.

By the time we ended praying for the last one, it was later than usual, and though the hijacked plane came to my mind over and over that night, I decided not to bring it up. (I "decided" not to obey the Holy Spirit!) We dismissed in prayer, and as we walked down the stairs from the prayer room, I distinctly remember saying silently to the Lord, "Lord, You are GOD—You can get those hostages free without our prayers, Father!" But it didn't happen.

All that week the cruel siege continued, while inside me, the need to pray with Doc and Irlene about the situation was growing so strong I could hardly wait to get up to prayer the following Monday night. I did pray about it by myself, but it was limited in power.

When like-minded people pray together on a regular basis over a long period of time, they move into close unity, and powerful prayers of agreement come forth under the leading of the Holy Spirit. Prayer becomes almost like a well-organized S.W.A.T. team moving in together to "take" their object in prayer. Scriptural UNITY in God's Will is the key. *"If two of you agree on earth as touching any matter, it shall be done for you of My Father in heaven."* (Matthew 18:19).

The Lord showed me once that a "Spiritual S.W.A.T. team" is a group to whom Special Wisdom About That is given, so they know exactly how or what to pray for a particular situation!

HE is the One who stirs up the desire in us and HE is the One who answers the prayers. *"For it is God who works in you, both to WILL and to do for His good pleasure."* (Philippians 2:13).

I believe God is seeking groups where HE can lead as He wills, not limited by man's pre-determined agenda or "subject" limitations already set in place. So many prayer groups meet for only specified or restricted prayer subjects, and they miss out on "the real action!" Plus God doesn't get "His" prayers prayed lots of times. The real action is in letting the Holy Spirit "give" the prayers and then just speaking them forth!

Anyway, the next Monday night, only the three of us were up in the prayer room again, and right away I told Doc and Irlene, "We've got to pray about the hostage situation and the hijacked plane!" and we started to pray! A Holy Ghost-breathed prayer is like a fire that jumps from one person to another and brings a "power focus" on the subject, somewhat like the sun's rays being focused through a powerful magnifying glass. Things get hot and things get done!

Almost immediately, the presence of the Holy Spirit filled the room. Doc and Irlene prayed in tongues while I paced the floor, and if it's possible to kick into "warp speed" in prayer, which it is, we did so that night! Oh, I get stirred up again in the spirit just remembering it!

As I walked and paced, it was as if, in the spirit, I was in the darkened cabin of the plane. First the prayers were for the passengers. I "saw" them sitting in their seats: weary, discouraged, and hopeless. Some appeared to be fitfully dozing, one man was lifelessly looking out the window, head propped in hand. I felt their hopelessness. Strong prayer went up for them in many ways.

Then I "saw" the hijackers. Two were standing in the aisles with guns in their hands, one facing the hostages, the other in back of them, guarding them from behind. They looked tired also, but they had a wild look about them. Then I "saw," clustered at one end of the cabin, other hijackers sitting more or less together, separate from the hostages. Then, in the spirit, I was standing beside them with my hands stretched over them, praying for them, The prayer the Holy Spirit gave for the hijackers was to bind and break spirits of suicide, death, and murder off them, also false martyrdom. That the Lord would give them a desire to LIVE; that they would start remembering their parents, sweethearts, wives if any, brothers, sisters, uncles, aunts, cousins and friends and would suddenly MISS them. That they would begin to LONG for them, long to see them and be with them; that they would suddenly want to LIVE.

The prayer precious Holy Spirit gave next was about the negotiations—for a new idea, a new solution, one in which *everyone* could "live and not die!" I "knew" in the spirit that God had at least one believer on the negotiating team, and strong prayer came forth for God's solution for this impasse, that He would give His plan to His child, the believer, and that He, our Heavenly Father, would receive the praise and glory for the solution among the negotiators (even if privately), since the solution came through His child. I was nearly hoarse by then, but not tired. The Holy Spirit anointing filled me and "carried" me.

I have summed up this prayer. By the time it was over, we KNEW it was done. God was answering that prayer. After briefly praying about some other prayer needs, we left that night rejoicing, eager to see the answer come forth, and to see GOD'S solution. I got home about 11 p.m., went to bed in faith, praising God for the resolution of the hostage crisis and went to sleep, not burdened by the hijacked plane situation anymore, praise God.

The next morning I was awakened about 7 a.m. by the news coming over Ed's alarm radio—the hostages were free! Sometime during the night (California time), the hijackers had surrendered with an agreement they would be flown to an undisclosed country and be released *with no charges*. This happened within eight to ten hours of our prayer. I know thousands of people were praying for the safety of the hostages, and I don't understand the dynamics of it; perhaps there were additional specific prayers the Lord wanted prayed so He could bring forth His full solution for everyone involved. From the resolution, I know God wanted everyone still remaining to live.

I also know "The anointing breaks the yoke." (Isaiah 10:27) and the prayer that night was anointed. I also believe the Holy Spirit showed what was happening in the plane.

There are so many prayer needs around the world, dear Reader, most of which we don't know about in the natural, but if you are a willing vessel, or perhaps I should say, an available vessel, God will use you to pray for some of those needs. If you are serious about deepening your prayer life with God, I recommend the book *Reese Howells, Intercessor* by Norman Grubbs.

After reading it years ago, probably in 1982-1983 (I carried it in my purse and read it over and over for about two years), I told our Heavenly Father, I was willing to be "hidden" all my life, if He would use me to pray for people and situations around the world. That I desired to pray for people I would never meet on earth, but who needed prayer, as well as those known to me or that He would send to me.

God has been faithful, and I have had great joy praying for people I didn't know in the natural, but who were revealed to me by the Spirit of the Lord. An infant left to die on a huge garbage dump in India who was appointed to be a great physician. Prayer for a missionary couple to find him, take him, and raise him in the Lord. I believe he will, or perhaps already has, come to America for his training, and probably Great Britain also, but return to India to serve his people. He will be known to the government for his great medical skills. That's the prayer the Lord gave. He is in his early to mid-thirties by now and very well could be a doctor already. Doc, Irlene, and I prayed together for nearly seven years, and I don't remember when it was that we prayed for his rescue and future.

For a Buddhist priest in his "cell," ready to give up because he had served Buddha all his life and was so empty he was about to end his life. Fervent prayer that he would not take his life, but would call out to God, "Whoever You Are!"—to make Himself known to him. That the Lord would reveal Himself to him and give him the courage to be His witness to the other priests, and no matter the cost (or opposition), in God's time, he would leave the temple to serve the Lord.

For a young man in prison, terrified of an expected homosexual gang rape—strong, urgent prayer for God's protection for him! That he would "Call out to the Lord!" for help and God would set angels around him to protect him, and also raise up Christian men in prison to befriend and "disciple" him, or teach him about the Lord.

These people were unknown to us in the earth realm, but precious Holy Spirit brought the images and situations so clearly, urgently, in vision as we prayed in the spirit with unity. We "stood in the gap" for them because they needed prayer, and we were set on praying the prayers the LORD wanted prayed and did not have pre-determined limits and designated subjects only about which we would pray. I expect Doc, Irlene, and I to meet all three of these individuals in heaven, along with many others the Lord led us to pray for, both individuals and various large groups. We prayed in faith, with unity.

After sharing praise reports, we usually opened the prayer meeting with a request or prayer along this line, "We have come, O Lord, to do Thy will, and Father, if there is anything or anyone in the world that needs prayer right now and doesn't have anyone to pray for them, let us pray for them! We are willing, Abba Daddy; we *want* to pray for them! Just show them to us and lead us by precious Holy Spirit, and we will pray whatever You show us for the situation or the person or people. We ask for the *privilege* of standing in the gap for them, Abba Daddy! In Jesus' Holy Name!"

The Lord never failed to answer our prayer. Sometimes it was for people and situations we knew about personally or through news reports or other ways, sometimes for ones we didn't know. There are innumerable things happening around us every day that are far beyond our natural experiences or knowledge. I know God has individuals and groups that move in bidding to His will who are changing lives, cities, and nations in Jesus' name, under the guidance of the Holy Spirit, but they cannot do it alone. God desires MORE people to give themselves to prayer and to pray for others.

I desire to stir in you a longing to move mountains and conquer giants in JESUS' name! This is my prayer for you, that when you see a need, you will not think about how big it is or how big the giant is, but your spirit will rise up, and with the invisible, but very *real* weapons of our warfare: faith, the blood of the Lamb, words (both God's and yours), the full armor of God, and the name of *JESUS*, you will march straight ahead, fearless, to the Land of the Giants and take back what was stolen from you or someone else—in Jesus' name! To God be all the glory!

"So I sought for a man among them who would make a wall, and stand in the gap before Me on behalf of the land, that I should not destroy it, but I found no

***one. Therefore I have poured out My indignation on them; I have consumed them with the fire of My wrath; and I have recompensed their deeds on their own heads' says the Lord God"* (Ezekiel 22:30–31). And *"I will declare the decree the Lord has said to Me, 'You are my Son, today I have begotten You. Ask of Me, and I will give You the nations for Your inheritance, and the ends of the earth for Your inheritance.'"* (Psalms 2:7–8). Hallelujah!**

Contacting the Author

If you would like to contact the author please write to:

Mrs. Donna Hamilton
P. O. Box 680096
San Antonio, TX 78268

or email Donna at:
wordofpowerprinting@gmail.com

Author's other books include:

Run to the Battle: *in Jesus' Name*
by Donna Hamilton

CPSIA information can be obtained
at www.ICGtesting.com
Printed in the USA
FFOW01n2028220217
32769FF